First World War
and Army of Occupation
War Diary
France, Belgium and Germany

61 DIVISION
183 Infantry Brigade
Worcestershire Regiment
2/8th Battalion
1 September 1915 - 31 January 1918

WO95/3060/4

The Naval & Military Press Ltd
www.nmarchive.com
Published in association with The National Archives

Published by

The Naval & Military Press Ltd

Unit 10 Ridgewood Industrial Park,
Uckfield, East Sussex,
TN22 5QE England
Tel: +44 (0) 1825 749494

www.naval-military-press.com

www.nmarchive.com

This diary has been reprinted in facsimile from the original. Any imperfections are inevitably reproduced and the quality may fall short of modern type and cartographic standards.

© Crown Copyright
Images reproduced by permission of The National Archives, London, England, 2015.

Contents

Document type	Place/Title	Date From	Date To
War Diary	Front Line W Of St Quentin	19/01/1918	21/01/1918
War Diary	Savywood	22/01/1918	25/01/1918
War Diary	Front Line W Of St Quentin	26/01/1918	30/01/1918
War Diary	Savy Wood	31/01/1918	31/01/1918
Heading	2/8 Bn Worcestershire Reg Sep 1915-Jan 1918		
Heading	61st Division 183rd Infy Bde 2-8th Bn Worcestershire Regt 1915 Sep-1918 Jan (1916 Feb, Mar, Apr Diaries Missing) To 182 Bde 61 Div		
War Diary	Maldon	01/09/1915	02/09/1915
War Diary	Epping	03/09/1915	25/10/1915
War Diary	Brentwood	26/10/1915	30/11/1915
Heading	War Diary of the 2/8th Battalion The Worcestershire Regiment From 1st December 1915 To 31st December 1915 (Volume 2)		
War Diary	Brentwood	01/12/1915	31/12/1915
Heading	War Diary of 2/8th Battalion The Worcestershire Regiment From 1st January 1916 To 31st January 1916 (Volume 3)		
War Diary	Brentwood	01/01/1916	31/01/1916
Operation(al) Order(s)	Operation Order No.37 By Col. Sir John Barnsley V.D. Commanding 183rd Infantry Brigade.	11/01/1916	11/01/1916
Operation(al) Order(s)	Operation Order No.38 By Col. Sir J. Barnsley V.D. Commanding 183rd Infantry Brigade	27/01/1916	27/01/1916
Heading	61 Division 183 Infantry Brigade 2/8 Battalion Worcestershire Regiment Feb, Mar, April Missing		
War Diary	Southampton	24/05/1916	31/05/1916
War Diary	France	01/06/1916	15/06/1916
War Diary	Riez Bailleul	16/06/1916	17/06/1916
War Diary	Croix Barbee	18/06/1916	21/06/1916
War Diary	La. Fosse	22/06/1916	30/06/1916
Heading	War Diary of 2/8th Bn Worcestershire Regt From 1st July To 31st July 1916 Vol 3		
War Diary	Fosse	01/07/1916	03/07/1916
War Diary	Laventie	04/07/1916	09/07/1916
War Diary	Faquissart	10/07/1916	15/07/1916
War Diary	Estairs	16/07/1916	20/07/1916
War Diary	Laventie	21/07/1916	24/07/1916
War Diary	Fauquissart	25/07/1916	31/07/1916
Heading	183rd Inf Bde War Diary of 8th Battn The Worcestershire Regt Augt 1st-31st 1916 Vol 4		
War Diary	Laventie	01/08/1916	05/08/1916
War Diary	Fauquissart	06/08/1916	09/08/1916
War Diary	La Gorgue	10/08/1916	17/08/1916
War Diary	Croix Barbee	18/08/1916	21/08/1916
War Diary	Neuve Chappel	22/08/1916	26/08/1916
War Diary	Riez Bailleul	27/08/1916	31/08/1916
Heading	183rd Infantry Brigade War Diary of 2/8th Worcester Regiment For September 1916 Vol 5		
War Diary	Moated Grange	01/09/1916	07/09/1916
War Diary	Riez Bailleul	08/09/1916	11/09/1916

War Diary	Grand Pacaut	11/09/1916	17/09/1916
War Diary	La Fosse	18/09/1916	30/09/1916
Heading	183 Inf Bde 2/8th Worcestershire Regt War Diary for October 1916 Vol 6		
War Diary	La Fosse	01/10/1916	01/10/1916
War Diary	Neuve Chappel	02/10/1916	07/10/1916
War Diary	La Fosse	08/10/1916	09/10/1916
War Diary	Croix Barbee	10/10/1916	13/10/1916
War Diary	Neuve Chappel	14/10/1916	20/10/1916
War Diary	Croix Barbee	20/10/1916	24/10/1916
War Diary	Neuve Chappel	25/10/1916	28/10/1916
War Diary	Busnettes	29/10/1916	31/10/1916
Heading	War Diary of 2/8th Battn The Worcestershire Regt For November 1916 Vol 7		
War Diary		01/11/1916	05/11/1916
War Diary	Rougefay	06/11/1916	21/11/1916
War Diary	Albert	22/11/1916	30/11/1916
Heading	War Diary 2/8 Worcesters December 1916 Vol 8		
War Diary	France	01/12/1916	31/12/1916
Heading	War Diary of 2/8th Battn The Worcestershire Regt January 1st To 31st 1917 Vol 9		
War Diary	France	01/01/1917	31/01/1917
Heading	War Diary of 2/8th Worcester Regt February 1917 Vol 10		
War Diary	France	01/02/1917	28/02/1917
Heading	War Diary of 2/8th Bn The Worcestershire Regt March 1917 Vol XI		
War Diary	France	01/03/1917	31/03/1917
Heading	War Diary of 2/8th Worcester Regt April 1917 Vol 12		
War Diary	France	01/04/1917	30/04/1917
Operation(al) Order(s)	2/8th Bn Worcs Regt Operation Order No.8	02/04/1917	02/04/1917
Heading	May 1917 War Diary of 2/8th Worcester Regt Vol 13		
War Diary	France	01/05/1917	31/05/1917
Heading	June 1917 War Diary of 2/8th Battn Worcestershire Regt Vol 14		
War Diary	France	01/06/1917	30/06/1917
Heading	2/8th Worcesters War Diary Vol 15 July 1917		
War Diary	France	01/07/1917	31/07/1917
Heading	Sept 1917 War Diary of 2/8th Bn the Worcestershire Regt Vol 17		
Heading	August 1917 War Diary of 2/8th Bn The Worcestershire Regt Vol 16		
War Diary	France	01/08/1917	11/09/1917
Map	Map		
Heading	October 1917 War Diary of 2/8th Battn The Worcestershire Regt Vol 18		
War Diary	France	01/10/1917	31/10/1917
Heading	2/8th Bn Worcestershire Regt War Diary Vol 19		
War Diary	France	01/11/1917	30/11/1917
Heading	December 1917 War Diary of 2/8th Bn The Worcestershire Regt Vol 20		
War Diary	France	01/12/1917	31/12/1917
Map	Sketch P		
Map	Patrol Map		
Map	Map		
Heading	War Diary of 2/8th Bn The Worcestershire Regt Vol 21		

War Diary Miscellaneous	France	01/01/1918	31/01/1918
Miscellaneous	Appendix VIII	12/05/1917	12/05/1917

Army Form C. 2118.

WAR DIARY
or
INTELLIGENCE SUMMARY.
(Erase heading not required.) 2/7 Batt Worcestershire Regt

SHEET No IV

Place	Date	Hour	Summary of Events and Information	Remarks and references to Appendices
	1918			
Front line W. of ST. QUENTIN	Jan 18		Trench routine. Casualties Nil.	4n J.63
	Jan 19		Trench routine. Casualties Nil.	4n J.63
	Jan 20		Trench routine. Lt Col LAWSON. A.B. Took over command of the battalion on	4n J.63
	Jan 21		returning from the course. Casualties Nil	
SAVY WOOD	Jan 22		Battalion relieved by 2/8 Batt Worcestershire Regt and proceeded to Hut & Hut area in SAVY WOOD. Relief complete by 8 P.M. Major ROWE A.V. took over command (temp) of The 2/4 Batt Glows Regt	K J.63
	Jan 23		Working parties. Q.M. Stores moved from GERMAINE to ETRIELLERS Casualties Nil	
"	Jan 24		Working parties Casualties Nil	4n J.63
"	Jan 25		Working parties Casualties Nil	4 J.63 4n J.63
Front line W. of ST. QUENTIN	Jan 26		Batt relieved 2/8 Batt Worcs Regt in front line. Relief complete 7.30 P.M. Casualties Nil.	4n J.63
	Jan 27		Trench routine. CAPT THOMPSON G.A. proceeded to DIV H.Q. Casualties Nil	4n J.63
	Jan 28		Trench routine. Evacuated 1 O.R.	4n J.63
"	Jan 29		Trench routine. 2/Lt HUTCHINSON A.N. and 3 O.R wounded while on patrol to stombs	4n Nil
"	Jan 30		Trench routine. Batt was relieved by 2/8th Batt Worcs Regt and moved back into support in SAVY WOOD. Casualties Nil.	4 J.63
SAVY WOOD	Jan 31		Working parties. Casualties Nil	4o J.63

M Lawson Lt Col

2/8 Bn.
Worcestershire
Regt.
Sep 1915 — Jan 1918

61ST DIVISION
183RD INFY BDE

2-8TH BN WORCESTERSHIRE REGT
~~JUN 1916 - JAN 1918~~

1915 SEP — ~~1916 JAN~~
~~1916 JAN~~ ⟹ 1918 JAN

(1916 FEB, MAR, APR DIARIES MISSING)

To 182 BDE 61 DIV

WAR DIARY or **INTELLIGENCE SUMMARY.**

(Erase heading not required.)

2/8 Mordell? Army Form C. 2118.

Hour, Date, Place	Summary of Events and Information	Remarks and references to Appendices
Sept 1 MALDON	Bn engaged in packing loading kits and preparation for moving to EPPING on Sept. 2nd.	Fine day
Sept 2	Bn proceeded by train at 11.45 from MALDON to BRENTWOOD and from thence by road to EPPING	Fine day, men cold.
Sept 3 EPPING	Bn engaged in arranging Camp and generally adapting itself to Camp life. Having had no previous experience.	Stormy day
Sept 4	Bn under Capt Griffiths went for route march reconnoitring areas	Fine day
Sept 5	Bn attended RC Divine Service on EPPING COMMON	Fine day
Sept 6 7	Bn exercised in outpost work by day and by night on air and ZEPPELIN heard steering CHESHUNT. Bomb heard in that direction.	Fine day
Sept 8	Bn exercises on Bn in attack on D1 area	Fine day

Army Form C. 2118.

WAR DIARY
or
INTELLIGENCE SUMMARY.
(Erase heading not required.)

Instructions regarding War Diaries and Intelligence Summaries are contained in F.S. Regs., Part II. and the Staff Manual respectively. Title pages will be prepared in manuscript.

Hour, Date, Place	Summary of Events and Information	Remarks and references to Appendices
Sept 8 EPPING	Bn exercised in Bde Field day, being Bn in reserve in attack from GILL'S FARM across COPPING'S BROOK to enemy's position in vicinity of COPPED HALL. Heavy explosions + sunfire heard in direction of LONDON, shells seen bursting in the air, enemy fires at Hostile aircraft.	Fine day
Sept 9	Bn exercised in attack, defence, A, B & C Cos in attack, D company in defence. On C.1 Area.	Fine day
Sept 10	Bn took part in Bde Field day on D.1 area. A,B,C & D Cos Park R of Bn exercises in attack 28th Woofers on left flank. Gen. Sir Ian Salisbury was present and afterwards inspected the Cars.	Fine day
Sept 11	Bn took part in Bde. General Parade on Epping Plain. Zeppelin passed over Bde Camp dropping bombs in Artillery ?/6 Photo lines, none of the aeroplane bombs exploded.	Fine day

(73989) W4141—463. 400,000. 9/14. H.&J.Ltd. Forms/C. 2118/10.

WAR DIARY or INTELLIGENCE SUMMARY.

Army Form C. 2118.

(Erase heading not required.)

Hour, Date, Place	Summary of Events and Information	Remarks and references to Appendices
Sep 12. EPPING	Bn. paraded at Bn. Divine Service Parade on EPPING PLAIN	Fine day
Sept 13	Bn exercised in attack Outpost on B4 area. C Coy in defence remainder in Attack	Fine day
" 14	Bn. took part in Bn. field day in B1 area. 28th Divn. is Present. Gen. Sir Alfred Codrington & Lord Salisbury watched the operation.	Fine day
" 15	Bn. exercised in Coy Outposts on D1 area and in night Outposts 6 D1 area	Fine day
" 16	Bn. exercised in Attack & Defence on A. area	Fine day
" 17	Bn. took part in Bn. field day. Outpost scheme HORSESHOE FARM to RIVETTS Fm in EPPING PLAIN	Fine day
" 18	Bn. took part in Ceremonial Drill in Bde. on EPPING PLAIN Bn. afterwards shields Fours	Fine day

WAR DIARY
or
INTELLIGENCE SUMMARY.
(*Erase heading not required.*)

Army Form C. 2118.

Instructions regarding War Diaries and Intelligence
Summaries are contained in F.S.Regs., Part II.
and the Staff Manual respectively. Title pages
will be prepared in manuscript.

Hour, Date, Place	Summary of Events and Information	Remarks and references to Appendices
Sept. 19 EPPING	Bn. attacked Bde. training scheme on EPPING PLAIN.	Fine day.
" 20	Bn. exercised in marching in pairs in EPPING FOREST by Company.	Fine day.
" 21	Bn. field day. Attack & defence of convoy near EPPING LONG GREEN. 2/1st, 2/8th WORCESTER attacking.	Fine day.
" 22	Bn. exercised in day attack on Bn. area. Concentration march & night.	Fine day.
" 23	Bn. exercised in outpost defence on C. Res. Motor car into B Coy. on patrol past midnight.	Fine day.
" 24	Bn. took part in Bde. field day on C+R area. 2/8th head of main guard. Lord Suffolk umpired.	Wet night.
" 26	Bn. attacked Bde. Communication trench in EPPING PLAIN.	Fine day.

Army Form C. 2118.

WAR DIARY
or
INTELLIGENCE SUMMARY.
(Erase heading not required.)

Instructions regarding War Diaries and Intelligence Summaries are contained in F.S. Regs., Part II. and the Staff Manual respectively. Title pages will be prepared in manuscript.

Hour, Date, Place	Summary of Events and Information	Remarks and references to Appendices
Sept 26. EPPING	Bn training. Route march to EPPING PLAIN. attenders	Fine day.
27	Bn engaged in field operations. Route march. A Company, one Platoon guards in B area	Fine day
28	Bn took part in Bde field day. Attacking a retiring enemy on EPPING	Fine day
29	Bn to proceed before a board of Sr. John MARR's on Territorial Scheme in Continuation of ammunition work	Very wet day after wet night
30	Bn took part in field day. Territorial Scheme in Continuation of Friday's field operations. Gen. Rd. Sadlier was present & criticised operations	Fine day

Francis Charlett
Maj
Comdg. 2/5 R Warwickshire Regt

Army Form C. 2118.

WAR DIARY
or
INTELLIGENCE SUMMARY.
(Erase heading not required.)

Instructions regarding War Diaries and Intelligence Summaries are contained in F.S. Regs., Part II. and the Staff Manual respectively. Title pages will be prepared in manuscript.

Hour, Date, Place	Summary of Events and Information	Remarks and references to Appendices
Oct. 1. EPPING	Bn. took part in Bde. Field day on Area B. Scheme set by Division. Men solely on march returns owing to rain.	Fine day.
Oct. 2	Bn. went for short route march returning owing to rain.	Wet morning.
3	Bn. attended Bde. Divine Service parade on Epping Plain.	Fine day, cold
4	Bn. engaged on outpost & protection of same on D area	Fine day, cold
5	Bn. took part in Bde. Field day, being Bn. attacking outpost line occupied by 1st Line other Bns. of Bde.	Fine day.
6	Coy. exercises indertaken in morning, Bn. by ½ battalion carried out concentration march on Tylers Green by night.	Fine day.

WAR DIARY
or
INTELLIGENCE SUMMARY.

(Erase heading not required.)

Army Form C. 2118.

Instructions regarding War Diaries and Intelligence Summaries are contained in F.S. Regs., Part II. and the Staff Manual respectively. Title pages will be prepared in manuscript.

Hour, Date, Place	Summary of Events and Information	Remarks and references to Appendices
Oct. 7 EPPING	Bn. holiday. Bn. sports in afternoon.	Fine day.
" 8	Bn. took part in Divisional Field day. Attack of enemy in position Epping–Cannonsbury. Dislodged of enemy & capture Cannonsbury; and pursuit of enemy retiring on new position. Cons. Salisbury in forest.	Fine day.
" 9	Bn. attacked some Co. Cons. of distrd. of Company Commanders	Fine day
" 10	Bn. attacked Divine Service on EPPING PLAIN	Fine day
" 11	Bn. marched with Bde. to CHELMSFORD and were billeted there for the night.	Fine day
" 12	Bn. in front of Bde. marched to HATFIELD PEVERIL. Bivouaced there for night in part of General Reserve to Division.	Fine day.
" 13	Bn. marched with Bde. into CHELMSFORD and was billeted there for the night.	Fine day.

WAR DIARY
or
INTELLIGENCE SUMMARY.
(Erase heading not required.)

Army Form C. 2118.

Hour, Date, Place		Summary of Events and Information	Remarks and references to Appendices
Oct 14	EPPING	Bn marched with Bde back to EPPING	This day.
" 15	"	Coys at disposal of Coy Commanders for purposes of intensive training.	This day.
" 16	"	Bn took part in Bde. Ceremonial parade on EPPING PLAIN	This day.
" 17	"	Bn took part in Bde. Divine Service parade on EPPING PLAIN	This day
" 18	"	Bn carried out attack through part of EPPING FOREST on D Area	This day
" 19	"	Bn took part in Bde. Field day, attacking Flying enemy in vicinity of COPPED HALL being in reserve and receiving fire from fire line	This day.

WAR DIARY
or
INTELLIGENCE SUMMARY.
(Erase heading not required.)

Army Form C. 2118.

Instructions regarding War Diaries and Intelligence Summaries are contained in F. S. Regs., Part II. and the Staff Manual respectively. Title pages will be prepared in manuscript.

Hour, Date, Place	Summary of Events and Information	Remarks and references to Appendices
Oct. 20. EPPING	Bⁿ carried out practice in final phase of the attack in D Area. C.O attended a Meeting of District Court Martial at CHELMSFORD.	Stormy day
21	Bⁿ practised attack through part of EPPING FOREST. C.O acted as President of G.C (Orwas) District Court Martial in DR. Woren the Camp of EPPING	Fine day
22	Bⁿ carried out attack & defence of Convoy on EPPING HARLOW R^d.	Fine day
23	Bⁿ fills in trenches near tents preparatory to strike Camp.	Wet evening
24	Wet day. No work on parade.	Wet day.

Army Form C. 2118.

WAR DIARY
or
INTELLIGENCE SUMMARY.
(Erase heading not required.)

Instructions regarding War Diaries and Intelligence Summaries are contained in F.S. Regs., Part II. and the Staff Manual respectively. Title pages will be prepared in manuscript.

Hour, Date, Place	Summary of Events and Information	Remarks and references to Appendices
25. EPPING	Bn left Camp at EPPING with whole of Bn + marched to BRENTWOOD and went into billets here	Fine day, cold
26. BRENTWOOD	Confusion at disposal of Company Armourers. Inspection of billets, ammunition - stores by C.O.	Fine day, cold.
27. "	Confusion under instruction of trained officers in bomb throwing. C.O. + Adjutant motored to BOREHAM in morning + attended lectures by Gen. Snow, Salisbury + afternoon at CHELMSFORD. Confusion lectures	Fine day, cold.
28. "		Wet day
29. "	Bn. took part in Divisional field day near MOUNTNESSING scheme of position, retiring from Sours through enemy force and taken up new position	Foggy morning

WAR DIARY
or
INTELLIGENCE SUMMARY.
(Erase heading not required.)

Army Form C. 2118.

Instructions regarding War Diaries and Intelligence Summaries are contained in F.S. Regs., Part II. and the Staff Manual respectively. Title pages will be prepared in manuscript.

Hour, Date, Place	Summary of Events and Information	Remarks and references to Appendices
Oct. 30 BRENTWOOD	Companies instructed in bomb throwing + coal leaves	Fine day.
" 31 "	Bn. afterwards Divine Service Parade at S. Thomas Church	Wet day.

Francis Clackett
Major
Comd'g. 2/8 Bn. The Worcestshire Regt.

CONFIDENTIAL

Army Form C. 2118.

WAR DIARY
INTELLIGENCE SUMMARY.

(Erase heading not required.)

Instructions regarding War Diaries and Intelligence Summaries are contained in F. S. Regs., Part II. and the Staff Manual respectively. Title pages will be prepared in manuscript.

Hour, Date, Place	Summary of Events and Information	Remarks and references to Appendices
Nov. 1. 1915 BRENTWOOD	Companies exercised behind by their own officers	Wet day.
2	Companies exercised in trench Manning. C.O. mentioned in	Fine day Cold
3	Companies exercised in trench Manning. BOREHAM in afternoon to see Col Low.	Fine day.
4	Companies exercised in trench Manning	Fine day
5	B" Took part in Divisional Field day being Bt" in reserve to 183rd Inf. Bd.	Fine day
6	Companies to front of Canton Commanders	Fine day.

WAR DIARY
or
INTELLIGENCE SUMMARY.
(Erase heading not required.)

Army Form C. 2118.

Hour, Date, Place	Summary of Events and Information	Remarks and references to Appendices
Nov. 7 BRENTWOOD	Bn. attended Divine Service at S. Thomas' Church BRENTWOOD	Fine day.
Nov. 8	Coys. under their respective C.O's for instruction in Trench Running, Bayonet Fighting	Stormy day
" 9	Coys. under their respective C.O's for instruction in Trench Running, Bayonet Fighting.	Fine day
" 10	Coys. under their respective C.O's for instruction in Trench Running, Bayonet Fighting.	Wet afternoon
" 11	Bn. took part in Bde. Route march BRENTWOOD INGRAVE BILLERICAY to BRENTWOOD	Wet evening.

WAR DIARY or INTELLIGENCE SUMMARY

Army Form C. 2118.

Hour, Date, Place	Summary of Events and Information	Remarks and references to Appendices
Nov. 12 BRENTWOOD	Coys usual routine. C.Os for letures. C.O. "ao," lectures to BOREHAM for ablution with Col. law.	Wet day.
" 13	Coys usual routine. C.Os for instructor in bomb throwing. Train R with C/Sgt Roll & Lieut Barron. Lectures & lgftrs & Machine Gun.	Fine day cold.
" 14	Bn attended Divine Service funeral of S. Thomas Church BRENTWOOD	Fine day cold.
" 15	Coys usual routine. C.Os in accordance with Co. programmes.	Fine day cold.
" 16	Coys carried out training in accordance with Co. programmes.	Fine day cold. but snow in mg/k.

Army Form C. 2118.

WAR DIARY
or
INTELLIGENCE SUMMARY.
(Erase heading not required.)

Instructions regarding War Diaries and Intelligence Summaries are contained in F.S. Regs., Part II. and the Staff Manual respectively. Title pages will be prepared in manuscript.

Hour, Date, Place	Summary of Events and Information	Remarks and references to Appendices
Nov 17. BRENTWOOD	Coys attend Returns and route march	Coys silver skill & rif.
18	Coys with Coy officers carried out their programme	Coys silver skill B/g
19	Coys under Company officers carried out their programme. C.O. w/c Sgt Davis & Sgrs Instrs to CHELMSFORD to attend Lecture on Musketry Regulations.	Coys snow skill & rif.
20	Coys under Company officers carried out their programme	Coys dry
21	Bn attends Divine Service parade at S. Thomas Church	Cold & dry
22	A Coy tools B Coy digging trenches for bayonet fitting C & D route marching.	Cold & dry

Army Form C. 2118.

WAR DIARY
or
INTELLIGENCE SUMMARY.
(Erase heading not required.)

Instructions regarding War Diaries and Intelligence Summaries are contained in F.S. Regs., Part II. and the Staff Manual respectively. Title pages will be prepared in manuscript.

Hour, Date, Place	Summary of Events and Information	Remarks and references to Appendices
Nov. 28. BRENTWOOD	Coy wore the C.O's Carried out their refective programmes. .303 rifles served out to A & B Contains Japanese rifles withdrawn.	Fine & cold
24	Coys under their C.O's carried out their respective programmes. C & D Companies served out with .303 rifles	Fine cold.
25	200 men of Bn. marched to MOUNTNESSING to dig trenches on London defences	Fine cold
26	Officers Boxing held a representation of Tournin Coy 1st time found	Fine cold
27	Bn. Commanded parade in march to BRENTWOOD Grammar School Grounds	Fine cold

Army Form C. 2118.

WAR DIARY
or
INTELLIGENCE SUMMARY.
(Erase heading not required.)

Instructions regarding War Diaries and Intelligence Summaries are contained in F.S. Regs., Part II and the Staff Manual respectively. Title pages will be prepared in manuscript.

Hour, Date, Place	Summary of Events and Information	Remarks and references to Appendices
Nov. 28. BRENTWOOD	Bn. attends Divine Service in S. Thomas Church	Fine cold.
Nov. 29 "	Coys under Company Officers carried out their routine programme.	Some rain.
Nov. 30 "	Coys under Company Officers carried out their routine programme.	Some rain.

Francis Chatterley Lt Col
Comdg. 9th Res Bn. The Worcestershire Regt.

(73989) W4141—463. 400,000. 9/14. H.&J.Ltd. Forms/C. 2118/10.

C O N F I D E N T I A L.

W A R   D I A R Y

of

THE 2/8TH BATTALION THE WORCESTERSHIRE REGIMENT.

from 1st December, 1915 to 31st December, 1915.

(Volume 2.)

Army Form C. 2118.

WAR DIARY
INTELLIGENCE SUMMARY.
(Erase heading not required.)

Instructions regarding War Diaries and Intelligence Summaries are contained in F.S. Regs., Part II. and the Staff Manual respectively. Title pages will be prepared in manuscript.

Hour, Date, Place	Summary of Events and Information	Remarks and references to Appendices
Dec: 1. BRENTWOOD	Bn. proceeded to MOUNT NESSING to dig trenches in LONDON defences. Owing to rain no work could be done	Wet day
2	B Coy exercises on miniature range. A. C & D carried out Coy programmes	Fine day
3	A Coy miniature range. B.C & D carried out Coy programmes	Wet day
4	Bn went for Route march to MOUNTNESSING returning by same route owing to flooded condition of main RID n road to BILLERICAY	Wet day
5	Bn attended Divine Service at S.Thomas Church	Wet evening

(73989) W4141—463. 400,000. 9/14. H.&J.Ltd. Forms/C. 2118/10.

Army Form C. 2118.

WAR DIARY
or
INTELLIGENCE SUMMARY.
(Erase heading not required.)

Instructions regarding War Diaries and Intelligence Summaries are contained in F. S. Regs., Part II. and the Staff Manual respectively. Title pages will be prepared in manuscript.

Place	Date	Hour	Summary of Events and Information	Remarks and references to Appendices
BRENTWOOD	Dec	6	D Company Miniature range. B Cy, Bayonet fighting. A + C Company Impromptu	Fine Evening
"	"	7	C Company Miniature range. A Cy. Bayonet fighting. C+D Company Impromptu	Fine morning
"	"	8	A Company Miniature range. B Cy. Bayonet fighting. C+D Company Impromptu	Fine day
"	"	9	B.N. marched to MOUNTNESSING to dig trenches	Wet day
"	"	10	C Bayonet fighting. D Miniature range. A + B Company Impromptu	Wet day
"	"	11	B.N. route march to HAROLD WOOD via WARLEY back to BRENTWOOD	Fine day
"	"	12	B.N. attends divine service at ST. THOMAS CHURCH.	Fine day.
"	13	11 a.m	Band of Epping in absence Pt A Barnes 4188 + declared a deserter	Fine day H.M.S
"	"	11-30am	" " " " n loss of equipment at Epping to EPPING CAMP.	

Army Form C. 2118.

WAR DIARY
— or —
INTELLIGENCE SUMMARY.
(Erase heading not required.)

Instructions regarding War Diaries and Intelligence Summaries are contained in F. S. Regs., Part II. and the Staff Manual respectively. Title pages will be prepared in manuscript.

Place	Date	Hour	Summary of Events and Information	Remarks and references to Appendices
BRENTWOOD	14.	9.A.M	Private A Bailed H188 having been apprehended by Civil Police at Insole in Surry was charged before the C.O. & remanded for Cmt martial	Wet day # M 60
	15.	12-30 P.M	Brig-General the Baronne of Salisbury, S.C.V.O.C.B.T.D. inspected all Regimental instates	Wet day # M 50
	16.	1.30 P.M	A detachment of this Battalion took over attached Air Defence Post at BILLERICAY from the 2/7th Leicester Regt	Fine day # M 58
		2 P.M	The General Amount Officer inspected all Transport Horses & this Battalion at Brentwood, SHENFIELD COMMON.	"
	17.		Four men forwarded to Provisional Battalion at CLACKTON & R.C.O & one man proceeded to 3rd Line Depôt 8.45 a.m. Sept Leicester Regt	Fine day # M 57
	18.	9-30 A.M 1-30 P.M	MALVERN LINK. Battalion Route March via HAROLD WOOD, NOAK HILL, SOUTH WEALD	Fine day # M 57
	19.		Divine Service Parade	Fine day # M 58
	20.	11 A.M	A District Cmt Martial was held at the COURT HOUSE BRENTWOOD for the Trial of Pte A Bailed H188. President Lieut Colonel Reeve 2/W Elsworth Regt	Fine day # M 57

Army Form C. 2118.

WAR DIARY
or
INTELLIGENCE SUMMARY.
(Erase heading not required.)

Instructions regarding War Diaries and Intelligence Summaries are contained in F. S. Regs., Part II. and the Staff Manual respectively. Title pages will be prepared in manuscript.

Place	Date	Hour	Summary of Events and Information	Remarks and references to Appendices
BRENTWOOD	Dec 21	2.15 PM	Sentence on Pte A Burke 41188 was promulgated on Battalion Parade. He was sentenced to 3.6 days detention. Brigadier General Th. Shopin of Salisbury received his farewell visit to Troops of the 61st Division.	Wet + Fog H.L.S
"	22		Major General R Barnardiston - Allison C.B. 77th n.u. Command of the 61st Division from indication Dec 21-1-5. Vide Battalion Orders 356. The Battalion 2nd Batt. Essex defiled the Divd Commander from 1.0. Battalion routine as usual	Wet + Fog H.L.S gti Fine H.L.S
	23			
	24	12 noon	Major General R Barnardiston - Allison C.B. inspected the Musketry after Range of the Battalion.	Fine H.L.S
		6.30 AM	Christmas hymns to all L.C. O's & men at HACKNEY UNION. Lieut Col F. Charlotte buried. Colonel Sir John Ramsay attended the Battalion.	
	25	9.15 AM	Christmas Day. A + B Coys attended Divine Service,	Showery H.L.S Fine H.L.S
	26	9 AM	C + D Coys attended Divine Service	
	27	9.30 AM -12 noon	Company Training. Remainder of day observed as a holiday	Wet H.L.S
	28	9.30 AM } 11 { AM	Battalion Drill at SOUTH WEALD, followed by Company Training	Fine H.L.S
	29		Company Training	Fine H.L.S

Army Form C. 2118.

WAR DIARY
INTELLIGENCE SUMMARY.
(Erase heading not required.)

Place	Date	Hour	Summary of Events and Information	Remarks and references to Appendices
BRENTWOOD	DEC 30.	9-30 2-30	Company Training. Visit of Colonel Stuart to Battalion.	Fine. H.A.S.
	31.		Company Training. Pvt. Turner. AE.3381. remanded to District Court Martial for Theft & escaping from custody.	Wet. H.A.S.

A. H. Griffiths Major
for O.C. 2/8th Worcester Regt

CONFIDENTIAL.

WAR DIARY

of

2/8TH BATTALION THE WORCESTERSHIRE REGIMENT.

From : 1st January, 1916.   To : 31st January, 1916.

(Volume 3.)

Army Form C. 2118.

WAR DIARY
or
INTELLIGENCE SUMMARY.

(Erase heading not required.)

Instructions regarding War Diaries and Intelligence Summaries are contained in F.S. Regs., Part II. and the Staff Manual respectively. Title pages will be prepared in manuscript.

Place	Date	Hour	Summary of Events and Information	Remarks and references to Appendices
BRENTWOOD	Jan 1	9:30 AM	Battalion Route March. CAPT. & ADJUTANT VIGORS returned from leave.	See H.A.S.
	2		Church Parade.	H.A.S
	3		LIEUT. COLONEL CHECKETTS President of a District Court Martial at BRENTWOOD	H.A.S
	4		" " " " " " " " " "	
	5		District Court Martial on PVT TURNER A.E. 3381.	H.A.S.
	6		Sentence of District Court Martial on PVT TURNER. A.E. 3381. Promulgated. 1/2 Bgo Battalion Medical Inspection.	H.A.S. H.A.S.
	7		CAPTAIN. DAVIES member of a District Court Martial Company Training.	
	8	9:30 AM	Battalion Route March. LIEUT. COLONEL. CHECKETTS proceeded on leave.	H.A.S. Leave
	9		Divine Service Parade. ST. THOMAS' CHURCH	H.A.S.
	10	8:40 AM	Company Training	H.A.S
	11	10 AM	Battalion inspected by COLONEL. M. DIXON, V.D. ex Officer Commanding Company Training	H.A.S
	12		Company Training	H.A.S
	13		Company Training	H.A.S
	14	9 AM	Recruits Company Training	Appendix A H.A.S.
	15	9:30 AM 7 AM	Company Training. A draft of 180 men from 3rd Line Depot arrived without previous warning. They were billeted & fed in DRILL HALL ONGAR ROAD LIEUT. COLONEL CHECKETTS granted sick leave.	H.A.S

Army Form C. 2118.

WAR DIARY
or
INTELLIGENCE SUMMARY.
(Erase heading not required.)

Instructions regarding War Diaries and Intelligence Summaries are contained in F. S. Regs., Part II. and the Staff Manual respectively. Title pages will be prepared in manuscript.

Place	Date	Hour	Summary of Events and Information	Remarks and references to Appendices
BRENTWOOD	Jan 16.16	9 A.M.	Church Parade	A.h.S.
		2-30 P.M.	"C" Coy changed billets from Tower Hill to Brook St. Village	
	17.		Battalion of Officer's Post at Billerica returned from duty. Company Training. All recruits medically examined	A.h.S.
	18.		Company + Recruit Training	A.h.S.
	19.		Company + Recruit Training	A.h.S.
	20.	2-30 P.M.	Battalion Inspected by Major G. Captain Vicars. M.V.O. transferred to 3/7th Essex Regt. General Dickson. Inspector General of Infantry	A.h.S.
	21.		Company + Recruit Training	A.h.S.
	22.		Company + Recruit Training	A.h.S.
	23.	9 A.M.	Church Parade. Captain Cliffe returned from Recruiting Duty.	A.h.S.
		12.45	Captain P.U. Vicors left battalion on transfer to 3/7th Essex Regt. Captain Davies took no duties as adjutant	A.h.S.
	24.		Company + Recruit Training. Sanitary Section inspected by Divisional Sanitary Officer.	A.h.S.
	25.		Company Training. All recruits from 3rd line Inspected by Major General R. Bannatine-Allason, C.B.	A.h.S.
	26.		Company + Recruit Training	A.h.S.
	27		Brigade Exercise Thorndon Park Fog.	Appendix 13 A.h.S.

1577 Wt. W10791/1773 500,000 1/15 D. D. & L. A.D.S.S./Forms/C. 2118.

Army Form C. 2118.

WAR DIARY
or
INTELLIGENCE SUMMARY.
(Erase heading not required.)

Instructions regarding War Diaries and Intelligence Summaries are contained in F. S. Regs., Part II. and the Staff Manual respectively. Title pages will be prepared in manuscript.

Place	Date	Hour	Summary of Events and Information	Remarks and references to Appendices
BRENTWOOD	Jan 28		Company + Recruit Training	A. & S.
	29	9.30	Battalion exercise, HAROLD WOOD, WARLEY, BRENTWOOD.	A. & S.
	30		Lewis Gunner Parades.	A. & S.
	31		Company Bombers + Recruit Training	A. & S.

Robert M Griffiths Major
for O.C. 2/8- Worcester Regt.

Appendix A

OPERATION ORDER NO. 37.
BY COL. SIR JOHN BARNSLEY V.D.   BRENTWOOD.
COMMANDING 183RD INFANTRY BRIGADE.   11. 1. 16.
Reference ½" O.S.Sheet 30.
----

1. On the night 13/14th January 1916 the 61st Division is billeted in the neighbourhood of BRENTWOOD. An invading force of all arms has landed at SOUTHEND and is moving on BILLERICAY with the apparent intention of cutting the LONDON main line of Railway.

2/1st R.F.A.Bde.
183rd Infantry Bde.
2/3rd (South Midland)
Field Ambulance.

2. A column composed as ~~under~~ per margin under the command of COL. SIR JOHN BARNSLEY V.D. will be at BILLERICAY at 11 a.m. on the morning of January 14th 1916, and take up a defensive ~~line~~ position to the S.E. of that town, delaying the enemy until the Division has taken up a defensive position along the main line of Railway.

3. The column will rendezvous at the road junction on the SHENFIELD - BILLERICAY road. East of point 166, at 10. 45 a.m.

2/1st R.F.A.Bde.

4. The 2/1st R.F.A.Brigade will proceed via LAWNESS. The remainder via SHENFIELD and HUTTON.

183rd Infantry Bde.
2/3rd (South Midland)
Field Ambulance.

5. The starting point for the 183rd Infantry Brigade and the 2/3rd (South Midland) Field Ambulance will be on the BRENTWOOD - INGATESTONE road, at the Junction of the INGRAVE road.

2 Companies 2/4th
Gloucester R.

6. The Advanced Guard, composed as per margin will be ¾ mile ahead of main body.

Headquarters
183rd Infantry Bde.
2/4th Gloucester R.
(less 2 Companies)
2/6th Gloucester R.
2/7th Worcester R.
2/8th Worcester R.
183rd Infantry Bde. S.A.A.
Reserve.
Brigaded Cookers and
Water Carts.
2/3rd (South Midland)
Field Ambulance.

7. The head of the column, order as per margin, will pass the starting point at 9 a.m.

8. The Brigade S.A.A. Reserve will be under the command of Major G.C.Gwynn, 2/4th Gloucester R.

9. The Cookers and Water Carts will be brigaded under an officer to be detailed by the Brigade Transport Officer.

10. Each Battalion will detail 2 cyclists to report to O.C. Advanced Guard at starting point at 8. 40 a.m.

11. All messages to be sent to Headquarters, at the head of the column.

(Sgd) M. Marriott, Major
Brigade Major, 183rd Infantry Brigade.

OPERATION ORDER NO. 38   *Appendix*   Copy No.

BY Col Sir J. Barnsley. V.D.   B.   Brentwood.

COMMANDING 183rd Infantry Brigade.   27/1/16.

Reference 1" O.S. Sheet 108.

---

	1. An invading force of all arms reached EAST HORNDON on the night Jan 26/27 & has taken up an entrenched position in the SOUTH end of THORNDON PARK.
2/1st R.F.A. Bde. 183rd Inf Bde. 2/3rd (S.M)F.Amb.	2. A Force composed as per margin under the Command of COL. SIR J. BARNSLEY V.D. is ordered to attack the enemy and either destroy or capture him.
	3. The place of assembly will be at SHENFIELD 10 a.m. at the Junction of the SHENFIELD - BILLERICAY road with the main CHELMSFORD - LONDON road by the second N in INN.
	4. The route will be SHENFIELD ‐ PRIEST LANE (the road cutting the D in BRENTWOOD) -SHENFIELD COMMON- INGRAVE GREEN.
	5. The strating point for 183rd Infantry Bde & 2/3rd (S.M) Fld Amb. will be on the LONDON- CHELMSFORD road at the cross road West of B in BRENTWOOD.
2 Coys 2/6th Glouc Regt.	6. The Advance Guard composed as per margin will be ½ mile ahead of main body.
	7. The Head of the Main Body will pass the strating point at 9-45 a.m. Order of march as per margin.
Hdqrts 183rd Inf Bde 2/6th Glouc R(less two Coys) 2/7th Worc Regt 2/8th " " 2/4th Glouc Regt. 183rd Inf Bde S.A.A. Res. 2/3rd (S.M.) Fld Amb.	
	8. The Brigade S.A.A. Reserve will be under the command of Major G.C. Gwyne 2/4th Glouc Regt.
	9. Each Battalion will detail 2 cyclists to report to O.C. Advance Guard at starting point 9-30 a.m.
	10. All messages to be sent to Headquarters at the Head of Column.

Sgd M. Marriott Major.
Brigade Major, 183rd Inf Brigade.

183rd Infantry Brigade. General and Special Ideas.
for Thurs, Jan. 27th 1916.

General Idea.   An invading force of all arms, advancing on BRENTWOOD from the South has reached EAST HORNDON on the night of Jan. 26th. and learning of the movement of troops in BRENTWOOD decides to take up an entrenched position on the South end of THORNDON PARK.

Special Idea.   The following troops billeted in BRENTWOOD and INGATESTONE are ordered on the morning of January 27th., to attack the enemy in THORNDON PARK, and either destroy or capture him:-

     2/1st R.F.A. Brigade.
     183rd Infantry Brigade.
     2/3rd (South Midland) Field Ambulance.

OBJECTS OF Exercise.

     Advance of Infantry covered by Artillery fire, maintenance of direction and touch, fire discipline.

     Place of assembly.

         SHENFIELD at 10 a.m.

61 Division
183 Infantry Brigade
2/8 Battalion Worcestershire Regiment
Feb, Mar, Apri Missing

WAR DIARY / INTELLIGENCE SUMMARY

Army Form C. 2118.

183/61
2/8th Argyll & Suth. Highlanders

Place	Date	Hour	Summary of Events and Information	Remarks and references to Appendices
SOUTHAMPTON	Aug 2/7	6.30 p.m.	10 Officers, 1 Sgt. R.A.M.C., 64 Artificers, 17 Cobblers & 9 Bicyclists sailed on the S.S. "Viper" for HAVRE	A.P.S.
		9 a.m.	2 Officers & 833 other ranks sailed on S.S. Duke of Argyle for HAVRE	
	2.5.	3.50 a.m.	S.S. Duke of Argyle arrived HAVRE. 2 Officers & 833 other ranks march to No.1 Rest Camp	A.P.S.
		5.15 a.m.	S.S. City of Dunkirk arrived HAVRE	
		4.10 P.M.	Battalion paraded & marched to Stn. entrained for D Coy + Orderly Room Sergeant issued to Point 3, HAVRE with all transport	
	6.	8 a.m.	Train stopped at ABBEVILLE 2 p.m. rem stopped ST. OMER. Battalion drew 1 Company detrained at MOLINGHEM at 4 p.m. & marched to ROEEOQ 7.30 p.m & billeted	A.P.S.
	7.	7 a.m.	Battalion inspection + billets inspected. Brigade Sports at 8 p.m.	
			D Coy arrived & billeted	
	28.		Coy/Div Orders addressed all Officers	A.P.S.
		5.20 p.m.	Lieut. General Sir. A.C.B. Haking K.C.B. Commanding 11th Inf. Bde at ST. VENANT	
	29.		18th Brigade inspected by General Sir Charles Monro, Commanding 1st ARMY	A.P.S.
	30.		Training with Company Officers. Musketry Park.	A.P.S.
	31.	7 A.M.	Battalion marched to LA FOSSE & billeted & billets	A.P.S.

Francis Churchill
Lt Col
Comg 2/8th Argyll & Sutherland Highlanders

Army Form C. 2118.

WAR DIARY
or
INTELLIGENCE SUMMARY.
(Erase heading not required.)

2/8th Worcester Regt

Vol 2

Place	Date	Hour	Summary of Events and Information	Remarks and references to Appendices
FRANCE	June 1.		Battalion attached to 105 Brigade for instruction. A Coy to 16 Cheshire Regt, B Coy to 15 Cheshire Regt, C Coy to 14 Gloster Regt, D Coy to 15 Sherwoods, in trenches at Neuve Chappel. A + C Coy in front line, B + D in support.	# A. 5
	2		Trenches for instruction	# A. 5
	3		Trenches for instruction	# A. 5
	4		Trenches for instruction	# A. 5
	5		Trenches for instruction	# A. 5
	6		Trenches for instruction	# A. 6
	7		Trenches for instruction	# A. 5
	8		Trenches for instruction. B Coy relieved A Coy	# A. 5
	9		Trenches for instruction. D Coy relieved C Coy	# A. 5
	10		Battalion left Trenches + marched to Riez Bailleul	# A. 5
	11	11.15 A.M.	2nd Lieut. Clements, + 45 other ranks, proceeded to Laventie for instruction with Tunneling Coy, R.E. Battalion took over trenches from 16th R.W.F. 113 Inf Bde, Right Sector, Moated Grange Section. Trenches C. Coy in support. Very wet, one gunshot 1 killed (accident) 2 wounded	# A. 5
	12.			
	13	10.45 PM 11.30 AM	From 2 p.m. Rain Heavy wind	# A. 5
	14	8.30 A.M.	Enemy bombing Party attacked Ducks Bill Crater. Our casualties 2 killed. 1 wounded Cratr recaptured 9-30 A.M. Rain all day. Line quiet.	# A. 5
		11. P.M.	Time advanced one hour	
	15.	12-1 A.M.	We exploded mine at M.34.O. Artillery supported, also Machine Gun + Riffle fire Burst. Enemy replied mainly with artillery till 1. A.M, Battalion relieved in trenches by 2/4th Gloucester Regt + went into billets at Riez Bailleul, one wounded	# A. 5

Army Form C. 2118.

WAR DIARY
or
INTELLIGENCE SUMMARY
(Erase heading not required.)

2/8th [Bn] W[est] R[iding] [Regt]

Instructions regarding War Diaries and Intelligence Summaries are contained in F.S. Regs., Part II. and the Staff Manual respectively. Title pages will be prepared in manuscript.

Place	Date	Hour	Summary of Events and Information	Remarks and references to Appendices
RIEZ BAILLEUL	June 16		Battalion at Rest	#2 5
	17	2-10 A.M.	Gas Alarm. Gas Plt slightly. Pro damage. Ventilation started To.	#2 5
CROIX BARBÉE	18	8-30AM to 1-2 P.M.	Funeral billets to CROIX BARBÉE	
		1 P.M.	Gas Alarm. Battalion stood to. No gas felt. 10-30 A.M. Church Parade	#2 5
	19		Posts + Working Parties	#2 5
	20		Posts + Working Parties. 2 Casualties (wounded)	#2 5
	21		Battalion moved to LA FOSSE	#2 5
LA FOSSE	22	8 P.M.	Companies under Company officers	#2 5
	23		Working Parties. Remarks under Company Officers Wiring. Bombing	#2 5
	24		Working Parties. Wiring + Bombing Parties in training	#2 5
	25		Divine Service Parade	#2 5
	26		2nd LIEUT. CHAPPEL returned to ENGLAND, sick. 2nd LIEUT. GASCOYNE transferred to TRENCH MORTAR BTY	#2 5
	27		Working Parties. 30 yd Rifle range under constructn. Battalion baths. W/t	#2 6
	28		Rifle Range used. Inspectn of Transport Parading by Brigade Transport Officer. W/t	#2 5
	29		Transport inspected by Lieut. Harrison, A.S.C. [COLONEL] W/t	#2 5
	30		Working Parties. Rifle Range. Bombing + Wiring. Capt. C. HOLCROFT returned to ENGLAND sick	#2 5
			Transport inspected by D.D.V.S.	#2 5

Francis Chickett [?]
Lt Col
Cmdg 2/8 [Bn] W[est] R[iding] Regt

CONFIDENTIAL.

WAR DIARY.
- of -
2/8th Bn WORCESTERSHIRE Regt.

From 1st July to 31st July 1916.

Vol. - 3.

Army Form C. 2118.

WAR DIARY
or
INTELLIGENCE SUMMARY.
(Erase heading not required.)

2/8th Worcester Regt

Instructions regarding War Diaries and Intelligence Summaries are contained in F. S. Regs., Part II. and the Staff Manual respectively. Title pages will be prepared in manuscript.

Place	Date 1916	Hour	Summary of Events and Information	Remarks and references to Appendices
FOSSE	JULY 1		Working Parties & Coy'ts drill	H.A.S.
	2		Divine Service Parade	H.A.S.
	3	12 n'n	Battalion moved to LAVENTIE & took over billets & posts from 2/1 Bucks.	H.A.S.
LAVENTIE	4		Working parties & posts	H.A.S.
	5		Working parties + posts	H.A.S.
	6		Working parties + posts	H.A.S.
	7		Working parties + posts. LIEUT. COLONEL F. CHECKETTS relinquished command & returned to ENGLAND. MAJOR L.L. BILTON, 17th ROYAL SCOTS took over command.	H.A.S.
	8		Working Parties + Posts	H.A.S.
	9		Divine Service Parade. 6 new officers arrived	H.A.S.
FAQUISSART	10	10 P.M.	Battalion moved to trenches at FAQUISSART & took over from the 2/7 WORC. REGT. Front line relief killed LIEUT. BALL & one man of B Coy killed, & 2 men wounded	H.A.S.
	11		Trenches. One man wounded. O.R.	H.A.S.
	12		Trenches	H.A.S.
	13		Trenches. 3 wounded O.R.	H.A.S.
	14		Trenches. 1 killed O.R.	H.A.S.
	15	5 P.M.	Trenches. B + D Coys relieved by 7th ROYAL WARWICK REGT. & marched to billets at ESTAIRS	H.A.S.
		8:30 P.M.	B & C Coys released 500 + similar in enemy's trenches. 3 O.R. wounded	H.A.S.
ESTAIRS	16	2:30 A.M.	A + C Coys relieved by 12th EAST. YORKS. & with H.Q. proceeded by motor lorries to ESTAIRS.	H.A.S.
		3-30 A.M.	B + D Coys on working parties. 3 wounded O.R.	H.A.S.

Army Form C. 2118.

WAR DIARY
or
INTELLIGENCE SUMMARY.
(Erase heading not required.)

2/8th Gloucester Regt

Place	Date	Hour	Summary of Events and Information	Remarks and references to Appendices
ESTAIRES	July 17		Working Parties. 2 O.R. killed 2nd Lieut Douro w.1. O.R. wounded.	A.h.g.
	18		Working Parties. 4 O.R. wounded.	A.2.3
	19		Working Parties. Major Bartlett transferred to 2/6 Gloster Regt.	A.2.5
	20	6 A.M	Battalion by Rte Bruars to Laventie to relieve all dets. M.A.B.5.6.	
		5.30 P.M	Arrived into billets Laventie	A.h.5
LAVENTIE	21		Rest + Working Parties	A.A.5
	22		Working Parties. 1 O.R. wounded.	A.2.5
	23		Stores Parade. Working Parties	A.2.5
	24	8 A.M	Battalion tel no trenches from 8th R. Warwick Regt.	A.2.3
	25		Trenches. 1 O.R. wounded.	A.2.5
	26		Trenches Lieut Tongden + 2 O.R. wounded 1 O.R. killed 1 O.R. wounded H.	
	27		Trenches The Wick Salient bombarded by artillery + trench mortars. 4 Officers joined from 3rd Line.	A.2.5
FAUQUISSART	28	8.30 A.M	Trenches killed O.R. 1. Wounded 4.	A.2.3
	29	10 P.M	Trenches Wounded 9 O.R. 2 Parties under Lieut Mitchell + 2nd Lieut Zeete entered the enemy's front line trench at N.19.A.4.72 + found it deserted + dismantled all returned safely.	A.2.5
	30		Trenches. 1 O.R. wounded.	A.h.5
	31	10 P.M	Battalion relieved by 2/7 Worcester Regt. + went into billets at Laventie, less A Coy in Posts.	A.h.5

J. Lawrence Lieut Major
Cmdg 2/8 Worc Regt

183rd Inf. BDE

War Diary
- of -
8th Battn. The Worcestershire Regt.

Augt. 1st — 31st 1916.

Army Form C. 2118.

WAR DIARY
or
INTELLIGENCE SUMMARY
(Erase heading not required.)

2/8th Worcester Regt

Instructions regarding War Diaries and Intelligence Summaries are contained in F.S. Regs., Part II. and the Staff Manual respectively. Title pages will be prepared in manuscript.

Place	Date	Hour	Summary of Events and Information	Remarks and references to Appendices
LAVENTIE	August 1		Rest + Working Parties. 1 O.R. Wounded.	A.A.S.
	2.		Working Parties. Capt. FRANKLIN. rejoined	A.A.S.
	3		Working Parties	A.A.S.
	4		Working Parties. 3.O.R. Wounded	A.A.S.
	5	12 noon	Battalion took over trenches from 2/7. WORCESTER REGT. 3.O.R. Killed. 1.O.R. wounded	A.A.S.
FAUQUISSART	6		Trenches Capt. TOWNDROW joined from Base. 3.O.R. Wounded	A.A.S.
	7		Trenches Patrol by C. Coy to Enemys Wire. 2.O.R. Killed 4th O.R. wounded.	A.A.S.
	8		Trenches	
	9	4-30 p.m.	Trenches taken over by 2/1 BUCKS REGT. Battalion moved into billets at LA GORGUE	A.A.S.
LA GORGUE	10		Rest + Baths	A.A.S.
	11		Companies under Company Officers	A.A.S.
	12		Companies under Company Officers	A.A.S.
	13		Divine Service Parade	A.A.S.
	14		Battalion Bathing at LE SART.	A.A.S.
	15		Brigade Horse Show + Sports	A.A.S.
	16		Battalion practice in Attack	A.A.S.
	17		Companies under Company Officers	A.A.S.
CROIX BARBÉE	18		Battalion moved up to CROIX BARBEE + took over forts on Reserve Line. No. 3195 SERGT. TROTH. awarded Military Medal	A.A.S.
	19		Working Parties	A.A.S.
	20		Working Parties. Divine Service Parade	A.A.S.
	21		Working Parties 1.O.R. wounded	A.A.S.

WAR DIARY
or
INTELLIGENCE SUMMARY.

(Erase heading not required.)

Army Form C. 2118.

2/8th Worcester Regt

Place	Date	Hour	Summary of Events and Information	Remarks and references to Appendices
NEUVE CHAPPEL	Aug 22-26	11.30AM	Battalion Held on Trenches from 2/7th Worcest Regt Capt. Barrow left for England & join Machine Gun Corps.	A & S
	23		Trenches. 2 O.R. wounded. Artillery bombardment of enemys trenches at 9.30.P.M	A & S
	24	12.30AM	Trenches. Bombardment of enemys trenches also 2.O.R. killed. 2/Lieut. Symons + 13 O.R wounded	A & S
	25		Trenches. Bombardment of Enemy's trenches at 6.P.M	A & S
	26		Trenches taken over by 14th East. Yorks.	A & S
RIEZ BAILLEUL	27		Battalion moved into Billets at RIEZ BAILLEUL. Ports taken over by 13 East. Yorks.	A & S
	28		From Above Parade. 2/Lieut. Simmons 2nd Lieut. Simmons arrived from BASE	A & S
	29		2/Lieut. Pritchard joined from BASE. 2/Lieut. Symons awarded the Military Cross. 1 O.R. wounded	12 & S
	30		Working Parties joined from BASE	A & S
	31		Working Parties Rain 2/Lieut. Cade joined from BASE Wet	A & S
			Rest.	A & S

J. Leonard Allen
Lt Col.

Vol 5

5.B

183rd Infantry Brigade

War Diary

of

2/8th Worcester Regiment.

for

September 1916

Army Form C. 2118.

WAR DIARY
or
INTELLIGENCE SUMMARY.
(Erase heading not required.)

2/8 Worcester Regt.

Place	Date	Hour	Summary of Events and Information	Remarks and references to Appendices
MOATED GRANGE	1916 Sept 1.	12 noon	Battalion took over trenches from 2/7th Worcester Regt. from Church Road to M.35.B.2.6.	# A.6
	Sept 2.		Trenches. 2/Lieut. Gumprey joined from Base.	# A.5
	3	12 n'n	Battalion handed over trenches from Church Road to Sign Post Lane to 1/8 York & Lancs Regt. & took over trenches from 2/4 Glos. Regt. from M.35.B.2.6. to M.19.d.9½.8. 2/Lieut Godsall arrived from Base.	# A.5
	4		Trenches.	# A.5
	5		Trenches.	# A.5
	6		Trenches. 2nd Anniversary on the formation of Regiment. 3 O.R. wounded	# A.5
	7	11 p.m.	3 Fighting Patrols under 2/Lieuts. Godsall, Teete & Robinson moved to German wire but were unable to enter trenches. 2/Lieut Teete & 1 O.R. wounded	# A.6
		10.30am	Battalion relieved in trenches by 2/7th Worcester Regt. & went into billets at Riez Bailleul.	# A.5
RIEZ BAILLEUL	8		Baths & Working Parties	# A.5
	9		Working Parties	# A.5 # A.6
	10		Divine Service Parade.	# A.6
	11		Working Parties. Battalion handed over billets to 2/5 Gloster Regt & marched to Grand Pacaut & took new billets from 2/1 Bucks. Regt. 2/Lieuts. Bellamy, Hull & Younghusband arrived from Base	# A.5 # A.5
GRAND PACAUT	12		Rest	
	13		Company under company arrangements	# A.5
	14		Battalion practice in attack.	# A.5

Army Form C. 2118.

WAR DIARY
or
INTELLIGENCE SUMMARY.
(Erase heading not required.)

2/8 Worcester Regt

Instructions regarding War Diaries and Intelligence Summaries are contained in F. S. Regs., Part II. and the Staff Manual respectively. Title pages will be prepared in manuscript.

Place	Date 1916	Hour	Summary of Events and Information	Remarks and references to Appendices
GRAND PACAUT	Sept 15		Battalion Route March.	#A.S
	16.		Working Parties. Presentation of Medals at MERVILLE by LIEUT.GENERAL SIR G. B. ANDERSON, K.C.B. 2/8 WORCESTER REGT. Guard of Honour.	#A.S
LA FOSSE	17.		Battalion moved into billets at LA FOSSE	#A.S
	18		Working Parties	#A.S
	19		Working Parties	#A.S
	20		Took over trenches Left sub sector NEUVE CHAPELLE from 2/7 WORCESTER REGT	#A.S
	21		Trenches	#A.S
	22		Trenches 1.O.R. wounded	#A.S
	23		Trenches 1.O.R. wounded	#A.S
	24		Trenches	#A.S
	25		Trenches	#A.S
	26.		Three Companies + # 2 moved into billets at LA FOSSE. C. Coy into billets at CROIX BARBEE	#A.S
	27		Working Parties	#A.S
	28		Working Parties + Baths	#A.S
	29		Working Parties	#A.S
	30		Working Parties	#A.S

A. H. Griffiths Major
for O.C. 2/8 Worcester Regt

Vol 6

183 Inf Bde

2/8th Worcestershire Regt.

War Diary for October 1916

Army Form C. 2118.

WAR DIARY
or
INTELLIGENCE SUMMARY.
(Erase heading not required.)

2/8 Worcester Regt

Instructions regarding War Diaries and Intelligence Summaries are contained in F. S. Regs., Part II and the Staff Manual respectively. Title pages will be prepared in manuscript.

Place	Date	Hour	Summary of Events and Information	Remarks and references to Appendices
LA FOSSE	6th October		Church Parade.	# 2. 5
NEUVE CHAPPEL	2		Took over trenches Right Sub Sector Neuve Chappel. Relief from 2/7 Worcester Regt.	# 2. 5
	3		1. O. R. killed	# 2. 5
	4		Trenches. 2/Lieut. C.F. Smith joined from Base	# 2. 5
	5		Trenches	# 2. 5
	6		Trenches	# 2. 5
	7		Trenches. Capt. Mitchell + 2/Lieut. Jones joined from Base	# 2. 5
LA FOSSE	8		Trenches taken over by 2/7th Worcester Regt. Battalion moved to Fosse	# 2. 5
CROIX BARBEE	9		Bn D Coy at Croix Barbee + B Coy La Gorgue	# 2. 5
	10		Rest.	# 2. 5
CROIX BARBEE	11		Battalion moved to Croix Barbee less B Coy	# 2. 6
	12		Working Parties	# 2. 5
	13		Working Parties	# 2. 5
NEUVE CHAPPEL	14		Took over trenches Right Sub Sector. New Chappel. Sector from 2/7 Worcester Regt less B Coy	# 2. 5
	15		Trenches 1. O.R. wounded	# 2. 5
	16		Trenches	# 2. 5
	17		Trenches	# 2. 5
	18		Trenches	# 2. 5
	19		Trenches 1 Officer 1.O.R. wounded	# 2. 5

Army Form C. 2118.

WAR DIARY
or
INTELLIGENCE SUMMARY
(Erase heading not required.)

2/8 Worcester Regt

Instructions regarding War Diaries and Intelligence Summaries are contained in F.S. Regs., Part II. and the Staff Manual respectively. Title pages will be prepared in manuscript.

Place	Date	Hour	Summary of Events and Information	Remarks and references to Appendices
NEUVE CHAPPEL	Oct 20	6:30 PM	Battalion relieved by 2/7 Worcester Regt & took over billets at CROIX BARBEE	# A. 5.
CROIX BARBEE			B Coy raid on S.11.A. 1/9.1.5 to S.11.A.3. 4/6. raid a complete failure but could not enter enemy trenches. Killed 11 wounded. Draft of 15 O.R. arrived from Base	# A. 5.
	21		Fine. Service. Draft of 55 O.R. arrived from Base	# A. 5.
	22		Working Parties	# A. 5.
	23		Battalion & Transport inspected by Brigadier General R.H. SPOONER	# A. 5.
	24			
NEUVE CHAPPEL	25		Battalion took over Trenches RICHT. SUB SECTION NEUVE CHAPPEL. from 2/7 Worc. Rgt.	# A. 5.
	26		Trenches	# A. 5.
	27		Trenches	# A. 5.
	28		Battalion relieved in trenches by 1st LONDON RIFLE BRIGADE & went into billets at CROIX BARBEE	# A. 5.
BUSNETTES	29		Battalion marched to BUSNETTES & billeted	# A. 5.
	30		Companies under Company Commanders. 25 O.R. joined from Base	# A. 5.
	31		Companies under Company Commanders	# A. 5.

J. Leonard Wilton
Lieut-Colonel
Comdg. 2/8th Bn. Worcestershire Regt.

Vol 7

War Diary
of
2/8th Batn The Worcestershire Regt
for
November 1916

Army Form C. 2118.

WAR DIARY
or
INTELLIGENCE SUMMARY.
(Erase heading not required.)

2/8 WORCESTER REGT.

Place	Date	Hour	Summary of Events and Information	Remarks and references to Appendices
	Nov 1, 16	9 AM	Battalion marched from BUSNETTES to FLORINGHEM & billeted for night.	# to S
	2		Battalion marched with BRIGADE to MAGNICOURT EN COMTE & billeted for night	# to S
	3		Battalion marched to BETHONSART.	# to S
	4		Companies under O.C. Companies trench digging	# to S
	5		Battalion moved to NEUVILLE AU CONNET & billeted	# to S
ROUGEFAY	6		Battalion moved to ROUGEFAY & billeted Wet.	# to S
	7		Wet. Battalion under Company arrangements	# to S
	8		Company Training. I.O.R. from BASE	# to S
	9		Company Training	# to S
	10		Coys Range firing. Coys at trenches	# to S
	11		Company Training. BRIGADE Staff Ride	# to S
	12		Divine Service Parade. Battalion Tactical exercise	# to S
	13		Company Training	# to S
	14		Coys Training. Rifle digging	# to S
	15		Battalion marched to LE MEILLARD	# to S
	16		Battalion marched to SURCAMPS	# to S
	17		Battalion marched to IF VALLE DE MAISON. Tate Fund & snow.	# to S
	18		Battalion marched to SENLIS. Wet	# to S
	19		Battalion marched to MARTINSART WOOD. Huts	# to S
	20		Working Parties	# to S
	21		Working Parties CAPT. C.W. HOLCROFT rejoined from BASE	# to S

Army Form C. 2118.

WAR DIARY
or
INTELLIGENCE SUMMARY.
(Erase heading not required.)

2/8 # Worcester Regt

1916

Instructions regarding War Diaries and Intelligence Summaries are contained in F. S. Regs., Part II and the Staff Manual respectively. Title pages will be prepared in manuscript.

Place	Date	Hour	Summary of Events and Information	Remarks and references to Appendices
ALBERT.	Nov 22		Battalion marched to ALBERT & billeted	# A. 3
	23		Working Parties	# A. 6
	24		Working Parties	# A. 5
	25		Working Parties	# A. 5
	26	7 AM	Battalion marched to MARTINSART WOOD & occupied huts. Very wet.	# A. 5
	27		Working Parties	# A. 5
	28		Working Parties	# A. 5
	29		Working Parties	# A. 5
	30		Bttn now Right Sub Section of Trenches from 2/1 Bucks	# A. 3
			Relief, & Supplies Regt for O.C. 2/8 Worcester Regt	

CONFIDENTIAL.
WAR DIARY.
2/8 WORCESTERS.
DECEMBER 1916.

WAR DIARY
or
INTELLIGENCE SUMMARY

Army Form C. 2118.

2/8 L.F. 15 Trench

Place	Date	Hour	Summary of Events and Information	Remarks and references to Appendices
FRANCE	Dec 1		Trenches from W MIRAUMONT Rd to SIXTEEN Rd. [DESIRE, REGINA, HESSIAN & ZOLLERN TRENCHES] 2 O.R. Killed, 1 man evacuated sick. 4 O.R. wounded & 2 gassed (Germans explosive)	By L.S. Disposition marked in APPENDIX A
	2		do. 1 O.R. Killed. 1 O.R. Wounded	
	3		do. 3 O.R. Killed. 6 O.R. Wounded	
	4		2 Officers Lieut Finch R.A.M.C, 2 Lieut Ladd wounded & duty 2 O.R. Killed 2 wounded	
	5		Battalion relieved in trenches by 2/7 WORC. and went into WELLINGTON HUTS about 1 mile north of AVELUY. 2 O.R. Wounded	
	6		Working parties to support & front line. 1 O.R. Wounded	
	7		do. 5 evacuated sick. 2 to BIBBS to ENGLAND	
	8		do.	
	9		do. 1 O.R. Killed 1 O.R. Wounded 3 evacuated sick MAJOR GRIFFITHS to ENGLAND	
	10		Handed over hut to 2/6 Manchester & went to huts in MARTINSART WOOD. 27 evacuated sick	
	11		Working parties to AVELUY SIDING & evacuated sick	
	12		Handed over to 2/4 Berks and went to billets in WARENNES.	
	13		Day of rest 1 evacuated sick	
	14		Conferences under O.C. Companies. Baths. 7 men evacuated sick	
	15		do 37 men evacuated sick Man	
	16		do 24 men received from Man	
	17		Church Parades. 6 men evacuated sick	
	18		Coy under training	
	19		do 4 men evacuated sick 6 men received from Man	
	20		do Clothes dampers 2 men wounded	
	21		do 2 men evacuated	
	22		Battalion moved to MARTINSART WOOD. Working parties	Yes
	23		Working parties	
	24		Working parties 2 men evacuated	
	25		Christmas Day. 2 hrs working parties. Dinners in evening	

J. Leonard Kellogg

Army Form C. 2118.

WAR DIARY
or
INTELLIGENCE SUMMARY.   2/5th Lincolns Regt

(Erase heading not required.)

Instructions regarding War Diaries and Intelligence Summaries are contained in F.S. Regs., Part II. and the Staff Manual respectively. Title pages will be prepared in manuscript.

Place	Date	Hour	Summary of Events and Information	Remarks and references to Appendices
FRANCE	DEC 26"		Working parties. 1 man evacuated	
	27		Working parties	
	28		H Q A & B Coys moved to WELLINGTON HUTS (W.12.d.3.3) C Coy to FABECK TRENCH (W.3.1.c)	
			D Coy to X.2.a. Cold & foggy. 1 man evacuated.	
	29		Working parties. Wiring in front of DESIRE TRENCH	
	30		Working parties. Wiring in front of DESIRE TRENCH	
	31		D Coy moved from X.2.a to W.2.d.c. 2/7th EDGE evacuated sick	Thus

J. Lovison Ellis
Lt Col

Vol 7

War Diary
of
2/8th Batt The Worcestershire Regt

January 1st to 31st 1917

Army Form C. 2118.

WAR DIARY
or
INTELLIGENCE SUMMARY. 2/8th Worcesters
(Erase heading not required.)

Instructions regarding War Diaries and Intelligence Summaries are contained in F. S. Regs., Part II. and the Staff Manual respectively. Title pages will be prepared in manuscript.

Place	Date	Hour	Summary of Events and Information	Remarks and references to Appendices
France	1917 Jan 1st		Relieved 2/7th Worcesters in Right Sub-section. Taking over same trenches as before (see Appendix A for December). 1 2 O.R. from Bunn all evacuated from hospital.	Apd.
	2nd		In trenches. Shelling heavy but no casualties. Weather dry 33°, but intense mud bad. 5 men evacuated sick	Apd.
	3rd		In trenches. Conditions similar. Having 9 front line pushed on	Apd.
	4th		In trenches	Apd.
	5th		In trenches. 1 O.R. killed (Serjeant Troth) 3 O.R. wounded. Small wiring party ambushed	Apd.
	6th		Relieved in trenches by 2/7 Warwicks and proceeded to WELLINGTON HUTS	Apd.
	7th		Marched from WELLINGTON HUTS to MARTINSART WOOD	Apd.
	8th		Marched from MARTINSART WOOD to billets in VARENNES. 9 O.R. from Bunn	Apd.
	9th		In billets at VARENNES. Baths. 112 O.R. from Bunn all from inoculation yesterday	Apd.
	10th		In billets at VARENNES. Baths. Training under Coy Commanders	Apd.
	11th		In billets at VARENNES. Training. 4 O.R. from Bunn	Apd.
	12th		In billets at VARENNES. Training. 3 O.R. from Bunn 3 sick evacuated	Apd.
	13th		do do 2 sick evacuated	Apd.
	14th		do do Church parade. 1 O.R. from Bunn 3 sick evacuated	Apd.

Army Form C. 2118.

WAR DIARY
or
INTELLIGENCE SUMMARY.
(Erase heading not required.)

2/8th Worcester

Place	Date	Hour	Summary of Events and Information	Remarks and references to Appendices
FRANCE	Jan 16		In billets at VARENNES	
	17		Marched to TERRAMESNIL about 8½ miles. Cold but fine	
	18		Marched to LE MEILLARD about 17 miles. Snowing very cold	
	19		Marched to LONGVILLERS about 6 miles. Training 15 sick evacuated	
	20		Marched to DOMVAST about 10 miles. Lost two ponies. Col BILTON had an operation 1/8R wounded sick Lieut PSON FORD joined from Base	
	21		In billets at DOMVAST. Front Batt 3 O R from Base	
	22		do do Church parade	
	23		do do	
	24		do Hard frost with cold wind Bills	
	25		do do	
	26		do Coted platoon training	
	27		do do	
	28		do do Platoon training 2/Lt NUTT joined from Base 1/8R	
	29		do do do 2 O R from Base	
	30		do do do 5 O R from Base	
	31		do do Church parade 2/Lt TETLOW from Base	
			do Training	
			do do	
			Rifles Lewis cold training	

H. Stimson Capt
In O.C 2/8 Worcester

10.B

Vol 10

February 1917

War Diary
of
2/8th Worcester Regt

Army Form C. 2118.

WAR DIARY
or
~~INTELLIGENCE SUMMARY.~~

2/8 r Worcesters

(Erase heading not required.)

Instructions regarding War Diaries and Intelligence Summaries are contained in F. S. Regs., Part II. and the Staff Manual respectively. Title pages will be prepared in manuscript.

Place	Date	Hour	Summary of Events and Information	Remarks and references to Appendices
FRANCE	1917 Feb 1st		In billets at DOMVAST. Very wet. Battalion training	
	2		do do do	
	3		do do do	
	4		Battalion moved into billets at ALLIEL near AILLY-LE-HAUT-CLOCHER, very wet	
	5		In billets at ALLIEL. Resting - weather very cold	
	6		do do Training do	
	7		do do do do	
	8		do do do do	
	9		do do do do MAJOR A.D. BARTLEET attached	
	10		Off a length In billets at ALLIEL do do	
	11		do do Church Parade. 3 men evacuated sick	
	12		do do Training. Wet very cold. 97 O.R. from Base	
	13		Transport proceeded by road. In billets at ALLIEL. Less wet.	
	14		Battalion moved by train from PONT REMY. Train left 7 am and detrained at WIENCOURT afterwards marching to DEMUIN. 4 evacuated sick	

WAR DIARY
or
INTELLIGENCE SUMMARY.
(Erase heading not required.)

2/8H Worcestrs

Army Form C. 2118.

Place	Date	Hour	Summary of Events and Information	Remarks and references to Appendices
FRANCE	Feb 16		Resting at DEMUIN. C.O. sent forward a Coy Commander to reat the KRATZ section of the line. And lent with the still fairly airtight. Battalion marched to FRAMERVILLE. CAPT CLIFF & LT EDGE joined from leave.	Ser 5 Ser 5
	17		Battalion took over right sub-section of KRATZ section from 2nd Batts 2/130th Regt of French Infantry. Line was held in 1 Coy in front line, 1 Coy in HIBOU & IRIS Trenches. 2 Coys at CARRIERES PARISON near LIHONS. Thaw commenced 59 O.R. from base.	Ser A Ser D Ser D Ser S Ser S Ser D Ser D
	18		In trenches. Thaw continued. Mud began to get bad. 1 O.R. evacuated.	Ser T Ser D
	19		In trenches. Took over part of line from 2/7 Worcesters. Line was then been us follows: 2 coys in front line, 1 Coy in GUILLAUME TRENCH, 1 Coy in HIBOU & IRIS. Mud very bad, being very great.	Ser D Ser D
	20		In trenches. Mud awful. Great difficulty in getting up rations etc. Mud still worse. Front line men/wounded also all C.T's	Ser D Ser D
	21			Ser D
	22		ats. Mud about same. Every they carried over top at night	Ser D
			11 evacuated sick.	

Army Form C.2

WAR DIARY
or
INTELLIGENCE SUMMARY. 2/1st Worcester
(Erase heading not required.)

Instructions regarding War Diaries and Intelligence Summaries are contained in F. S. Regs., Part II. and the Staff Manual respectively. Title pages will be prepared in manuscript.

Place	Date	Hour	Summary of Events and Information	Remarks and references to Appendices
FRANCE	First			
	24		In trenches. Slight improvement but things very bad. Enemy shelled transport every but did no damage. 12 evacuated sick.	Flass FIRSD
	25		In trenches. About the same. 6 in artillery action in evening. 32 evacuated sick.	FIRSD Flass
	26		In trenches. Relieved at night by 2/5th WAR WICKS. Relief complete at 2.20 am.	Flass
	27		In billets at VAUVILLERS. Raining 9.0 to 8 pm. 2/Lt. HOBSON joined for duty.	Flass FIRSD
	28		do. do. Training. Weather milder & finer.	Flass FIRSD

ILB Stevens Capt
6.C. 2/1st Worcester
for

Vol XI

March 1917
—
War Diary
- of -
2/8th Bn. The Worcestershire Regt
———

11·B

Army Form C. 2118.

WAR DIARY
or
INTELLIGENCE SUMMARY.
(Erase heading not required.)

2/8th WORCESTERS

Instructions regarding War Diaries and Intelligence Summaries are contained in F. S. Regs., Part II. and the Staff Manual respectively. Title pages will be prepared in manuscript.

Place	Date	Hour	Summary of Events and Information	Remarks and references to Appendices
FRANCE	1st Aug		In billets at VAUVILLERS. Coy training. 20 R evacuated	
	2		do	
	3		do	
	4		do Battalion attack. 4 OR evacuated	
	5		do Church parade	
	6		do Training. 8 OR from Base. 1 OR evacuated	
	7		do Training	
	8		do Inoculation of the battalion practically finished	
			1 OR evacuated	
	9		Battalion moved into billets at FRAMERVILLE. 2 evacuated	
			B & C Coys moved to CARRIÈRES, PARISON. Trench training	
			1 evacuated	
	10		In FRAMERVILLE & PARISON. Special training	
	11		do Church parade	
	12		do Working parties & special training	
	13		Lt ERNITSHELL joined from base	
			In FRAMERVILLE & PARISON	

Army Form C. 2118.

WAR DIARY
or
INTELLIGENCE SUMMARY.
(Erase heading not required.)

2/8th Worcesters

Place	Date	Hour	Summary of Events and Information	Remarks and references to Appendices
FRANCE	March 14th		Took over line from 2/7th Worcesters stretching from REPOS TRENCH to LIHONS - CHAULNES road. 3 companies in line, 1 in outpost, Relief finished at 7 am. 15th. 3 OR evacuated sick.	
	15		In line. Very windy. Little shelling. Patrols found line held.	
	16		In line, rather misty. Patrols found line still held.	
	17		In line. At about 5 pm we found enemy line unoccupied, moved men and established posts. 4 OR wounded by a bomb. Otherwise no enemy seen. 2 OR evacuated sick. Patrols pushed through CHAULNES.	
	18		At 10 am battalion advanced and occupied line of trenches near HYENCOURT LE-GRAND running out on 170.5 (?) to BERSAUCOURT. Wings & advanced parties & warned. 4 men evacuated sick.	
	19		Battalion advanced to DRESLINCOURT. Billeting in village. Rain all night.	
	20		In billets at DRESLINCOURT. 16 OR evacuated sick.	
	21		do. Work in nature of cross roads, bridges and not.	
	22		do. do. 12 evacuated sick.	
	23		do. do.	

WAR DIARY
or
INTELLIGENCE SUMMARY.
(Erase heading not required.)

Army Form C. 2118.

Place	Date	Hour	Summary of Events and Information	Remarks and references to Appendices
FRANCE	Aug 25		In billets at DRESLINCOURT. Work on wire and in digging line on west bank of SOMME	
	25		Moved to POTTE. Work on wire and SOMME trench. 2 Lt Chevalier Ur jun lieu, 2 Lt L'ETETE left from Flying Corps.	
	26		In POTTE. Working on wire.	
	27		Moved to CROIX MOLIGNAUX on east bank of SOMME. Work in galleries	
	28		Took over line with 2 companies in VILLEVEQUE & 2 companies with HY at TREFCON. Ordy all right. Know and saw.	
	29		In line. No shelling on our line but telescopes of enemy. Moved Batn H.Q. to VILLEVEQUE	
	30		and during the night advanced our line to MARTEVILLE. No opposition. Day strong posts which were down rather heavily shelled late in the day. 4 o.r. Evacuated Sick	6 Casualties
	31st		Posts heavily shelled. Wire all posts in & consolidated	

J. Abram Kelly
Major
Comdg 2/5 Worc. Rgt.

12.B

Vol 12

April 1917

War Diary
of
2/8th Worcester Regt

Army Form C. 2118.

WAR DIARY
or
INTELLIGENCE SUMMARY.
(Erase heading not required.)

Instructions regarding War Diaries and Intelligence Summaries are contained in F. S. Regs., Part II. and the Staff Manual respectively. Title pages will be prepared in manuscript.

Place	Date	Hour	Summary of Events and Information	Remarks and references to Appendices
FRANCE			Reference MAPS 62c & 62b 1/40000	
	1/4/17	1.30 am	A strong patrol under Lt. D.R. BOMFORD proceeded to ATILLY and patrolled the outskirts of the town.	
			Enemy sentry groups opened heavy fire your replied.	2 casualties
		10 am	Battalion relieved by 2/7 Worcesters. (Relief complete 11:40 am) and returned to MONCHY LAGACHE	
	2/4/17	8 am	Unexpected order to move up again to VILLEVÊQUE and relieve 2/4 Glosters (relief complete 10.30 am) Major R.M DANKS, 2/Lt F.H. HEYWORTH, 2/Lt W.G. TURNER & O.R.s joined	Operation Order No.8
			2/7 Worcesters have advanced. Operation Order No.8 issued (copy attached).	
		2.30 pm	Enemy has not waited for the attack. Battalion push on to support Civilian between VILLEVÊQUE and MARTÉVILLE. Invited Infantry Report for VILLEVÊQUE. Heavy rain.	
	3/4/17		Broke in roads. Repaired as yesterday. Infantry Report. Shelter & build for men.	
	4/4/17		Took over the line from 7th Worcesters. 1 Company in MAISSEMY 1 Company in VILLECHOLES 1 Company in trenches on the Ridge at Mon de VILLECHOLES 1 Company in shelters on the VERMAND – ST QUENTIN Road. Relief complete 6.30 pm.	
				2/Lt R.C.P. Hodgson admitted to Hospital.
	5/4/17	12 midnight	Pushed forward pickets to BOIS de CARTENOY and established a post there. Heavy snowstorm. Established another post in BOIS de CARTENOY. Allied Battalion line of resistance is—	
			General line MAISSEMY – MAISON de GARDE	
				14 O.R's evacuated
	6/4/17	11.45 pm	Battalion attacked Hill 120 [62c M 14 b and d] this and a half Companies on the attack.	6 O.R's evacuated 1 wounded
			Attack successful on right flank. Left flank held up and driven back by M.G. fire.	

Army Form C. 2118.

WAR DIARY
or
INTELLIGENCE SUMMARY.
(Erase heading not required.)

Instructions regarding War Diaries and Intelligence Summaries are contained in F.S. Regs., Part II. and the Staff Manual respectively. Title pages will be prepared in manuscript.

Place	Date	Hour	Summary of Events and Information	Remarks and references to Appendices
France	3/4/17	2.30am	Attacked again on left flank and consolidated a line of Red - ground Trenches. Attack by 182nd Bde on our right unsuccessful. 12 O.R. wounded. 1/Lt N. Bamford wounded. 3 O.R. wounded	
	8/4/17	11.15pm	Relieved by 5th Warwicks and marched out to TERTRY and MONCHY-LAGACHE. Capt A.V. Frow + 1 O.R. rejoined from England	
	9/4/17	3.30pm	1 Company Bd Hdqrs at TERTRY. 3 Companies at MONCHY-LAGACHE. 1 O.R. wounded	
			Moved to ATHIES joining our own 35th Division. Capt Tomlin (C.F.) admitted to Hospital	
	10/4/17		Batta. + riflemen. Nothing on paper. 2/Lt E.H.A. Lockwood + 2/Lt A.J. Butler + 2 O.R. joined from base	
	11/4/17		2 Companies working on roads. 2 Companies training	6 O.R. joined from base.
	12/4/17		3 " " " " " " "	1 O.R. evacuated to C.C.S.
	13/4/17		3 " " " " " " "	
	14/4/17		3 " " " " " " "	1 O.R. evacuated to C.C.S.
	15/4/17		2 " " " " " " "	1 O.R. evacuated to C.C.S. and church parade service
	16/4/17		2 " " " " " " "	1 O.R. joined from base
	17/4/17		Batta. training and attack practice	
	18/4/17		2 Companies working on roads. 2 Companies training	2/Lt J. Nott admitted to hospital. 6/Lt W.H. Cornelius-Raine do. Capt R.D. Moore Rank joined
	19/4/17		4 " " " " " " "	21 O.R. evacuated to C.C.S.
	20/4/17		4 " " " " " " "	Batta drill. Sgt Tarrant, Sgt George, Pte Parsons, awarded military medal by Corps Commander

Army Form C. 2118.

T2134. Wt. W708—776. 500000. 4/15. Sir J. C. & S.

Army Form C. 2118.

WAR DIARY
or
INTELLIGENCE SUMMARY.
(Erase heading not required.)

Instructions regarding War Diaries and Intelligence Summaries are contained in F.S. Regs., Part II. and the Staff Manual respectively. Title pages will be prepared in manuscript.

Place	Date	Hour	Summary of Events and Information	Remarks and references to Appendices
FRANCE	21/4/17	11:30 a.m.	Batt. marched from ATHIES to GERMAINE, transpt to la FOREST. Casualties 32 Others	
			4 Co. working on roads before noon.	
	22/4/17		Batt. working clearing of billets and billeting area. 1 O.R. evacuated C.C.S.	
	23/4/17		do. do. and Batt. drill. 12 O.R. to C.C.S.	
	24/4/17		do. do. 10 R. evacuated to transportation	
	25/4/17		4 Co. working parties on roads. Batt. drill. 15 O.R. joined unit from base.	
	26/4/17		Batt. parade and attack practice.	
	27/4/17		Working parties. Afternoon sports.	
	28/4/17		Batt. parade and attack practice. C.S.M. CHAD. Sgt. STANTON & L/Sgt. STANTON awarded parchments. 3/Lt F.A. ADAMS (6 "Novices") joined from Base. 11 O.R. joined from base	
	29/4/17		Church parade. 3/Lt F.A. ADAMS (6 "Novices") joined from Base. 11 O.R. joined from base	
	30/4/17		Batt. parade and attack practice. 29/3/17 G. PRITCHARD & LtR H. STALLARD awarded MILITARY CROSS	

V. Leonard Billingley
Lt Col
cmdg 7th Somerset Rgt

2/8th Br. Worcs. Regt.

Operation Order No 8

Ref. 1/40,000 Map 62c.

1. The 61st Div will establish itself this evening at MAISSEMY and on the Ridge S. of that Town, thence via Road Junction R.36.d.7.2 to join up with the 32nd Div at X ROADS S.2.a.6.3.

2. The 183 Bde will attack with 3 Battalions, 2/8th Worcesters in Reserve.

3. The attack will start at 3 p.m. today.

4. Objectives will be as follows:-

   6th Glosters The Ridge from R.36.c.8.2. to Road Junction R.30.a.1.1.

   4th Glosters The Ridge from R.30.a.1.1. to R.33.d.7.5.

   7th Worcesters Point R.23.d.7.5 to MAISSEMY inclusive

   8th Worcesters Reserve at VILLEVEQUE.

5. DRESS - Fighting Order (6 Flares for Signalling to Aeroplanes will be carried by each Platoon)

6. ADVANCED DRESSING STATION VILLEVEQUE.

7. Bn Hdqrs:- VILLEVEQUE in the dug-out at W.12.d.7.9 where all reports will be sent

Issued at 11.30 a.m

Copy No 1 War Diary.
     2 O.C. A Coy
     3   " B "
     4   " C "
     5   " D "
     6 R.S.M.
     7 Bn HQ
     8 Spare.

L. Leonard Sutton
Lieut-Col.
Cmdg. 2/8 Worcs. Regt

2/4/17

Vol 13

May 1917

War Diary

of

2/8th Worcester Regt.

Lobby 13.B

13.B

WAR DIARY
INTELLIGENCE SUMMARY. 2/8 WORCESTERSHIRE REG.T

(Erase heading not required.)

Army Form C. 2118.

Ref Map 62° 1: 40,000

Place	Date	Hour	Summary of Events and Information	Remarks and references to Appendices
FRANCE	1917 May 1		Inspection by Major Gen.l MacKenzie C.B. Cmdg 61st Division and presentation of Parchment to C.S.M. CHAD Sg.t STANTON and L/Cpl SPAWTON	
	2		Battalion move to Brigade Reserve on the railway cutting and sunken pit at ATTILLY [X.10.b.3.1.] Relieved 2/4 Oxford & Bucks relief complete 11.40am 1 OR evacuated to C.C.S.	Appendix C.
	night 2/3		Forward change of own patrols at HOLNON on the line of resistance & starch mining the BROWN LINE (see attached plan)	
	3rd		Continued wiring on BROWN LINE. 1 OR evacuated to C.C.S. 2/Lt K.B.TETLOW to Hospital 2/Lt C.A. UNDERWOOD joined from Base	
	4th		Continued wiring on BROWN LINE 1 OR evacuated to C.C.S	
	5th		— do — 1.O.R " "	
	6th		Relieved 2/7 WORCESTERS in Left support. 1 Company attached to 2/7th Worc.s in close support 1 officer & other ranks. Relief complete 9.40 pm 7 OR joined from Base. 3 OR evacuated to C.C.S.	
	6th		Patrol working at night & wiring BROWN LINE	
	7th		" by day & night " "	
	8th		" " " " "	2/Lt C.F.S.C. CLEMENTS proceeded to Base [Auth D.G.R 2281/258-]

Army Form C. 2118.

WAR DIARY
INTELLIGENCE SUMMARY.
(Erase heading not required.)

2/8 WORCESTERSHIRE REG.T (T.F.)

Instructions regarding War Diaries and Intelligence Summaries are contained in F. S. Regs., Part II. and the Staff Manual respectively. Title pages will be prepared in manuscript.

Place	Date	Hour	Summary of Events and Information	Remarks and references to Appendices
FRANCE	1917 May 9		Sortees digging by day mostly on BLUE & BROWN LINES	
	10		" " " " " " and on support line	
	11		2/Lt FARMER & 7 O.R. wounded (3 remained at duty) 2 O.R. from Base	
			Sortees digging by day on BROWN LINE and by night on FAYET support line. Lt T.N. HURRELL struck off strength posted to 61 M.T.M.B. (auth. D.A.G. 2679/9 of 30.4.17	
	12		do- 1. O.R. evacuated to C.C.S.	
	13		-d- 2/Lt R.C.F. HODGSON reported from Base. 2 O.R. wounded	
	14		-d- 1. O.R. Wounded.	
	15		Battalion relieved by 2/ 139th French Inf. Regt. Relief complete 2.10 am 16/5/17	
	16		Battalion marched to GERMAINE.	
			Battalion at GERMAINE.	
	17		" marched to MESNIL-ST-NICAISE	
	18		" " NESLE and entrained arrived at LONGUEAU and marched	
			to BERTANGLES 6. O.R. evacuated to C.C.S.	
	19		Companies under Company Commanders	

Army Form C. 2118.

WAR DIARY
or
INTELLIGENCE SUMMARY.
(Erase heading not required.)

Instructions regarding War Diaries and Intelligence Summaries are contained in F.S. Regs., Part II. and the Staff Manual respectively. Title pages will be prepared in manuscript.

Place	Date	Hour	Summary of Events and Information	Remarks and references to Appendices
FRANCE	1917 May 20	11am	Battalion Church Parade.	
		4.30p	Transport arrived from GERMAINE, 2 O.R evacuated to C.C.S	
	21		Battalion marched to billets at BEAUVAL. S.O.R evacuated to Stat. Hospital	
	22		Brigade drill - Battn.	
	23		Battalion marched to billets at SUS-ST-LEGER. MAJOR R.M. DANKS proceeded to ENGLAND. 7 O.R evacuated to C.C.S	
	24		Battalion marched to LARBRET, entrained there and proceeded to ARRAS & billeted at SCHRAMM Barracks	
	25		Rest - clean up. 2 O.R evacuated to C.C.S	
	26		Training. 1 O.R evacuated to C.C.S. 1 O.R received from Base	
	27	10.15	Church Parade - Training. I.O.B to Adv? Transport Depot ABBEVILLE	
	28		Battalion in attack (Church Church) at PETIT CHATEAU near WAILLY. The following have been "mentioned in Despatches" in SIR DOUGLAS HAIG'S despatch of April 9th. Serjt. Lieut. Col. L.L. BILTON. 240705 C.S.M EAMES T.H. 240754 C.S.M. JENKINS. A. 240705 C.Q.M.S MICKLING F.H. 2 O.R evacuated to C.C.S	
	29		Training. C9 Comrades recovered support area near BOIS-DES-BOEUFS - TILLOY	

Army Form C. 2118.

WAR DIARY
or
INTELLIGENCE SUMMARY.
(Erase heading not required.)

Instructions regarding War Diaries and Intelligence Summaries are contained in F. S. Regs., Part II. and the Staff Manual respectively. Title pages will be prepared in manuscript.

Place	Date	Hour	Summary of Events and Information	Remarks and references to Appendices
FRANCE	30.5.17		Training. Acting C.O. & staff reconnoitred support area near BOIS-DES-BOEUFS – TILLOY. 2.O.R. to ENGLAND for Commission.	
"	31.5.17		Training. CAPT A. CLIFF proceeded to Div. Burial Party.	

T2134. Wt. W708—776. 500000. 4/15. Sir J. C. & S.

Vol 14

June 1917.

War Diary

of

2/8th Battn Worcestershire Regt

Army Form C. 2118.

WAR DIARY
or
INTELLIGENCE SUMMARY.
(Erase heading not required.)   2/8TH BN WORCESTERSHIRE REGT (T.F.)

Instructions regarding War Diaries and Intelligence Summaries are contained in F.S. Regs., Part II. and the Staff Manual respectively. Title pages will be prepared in manuscript.

Place	Date	Hour	Summary of Events and Information	Remarks and references to Appendices
FRANCE	1.6.17	6.pm	Battalion moved into Bde Support at BOIS-DES-BOEUFS and 6th row from the	
			2/4th BERKS. Relief completed 9.45 p.m. 1 O.R. evacuated to C.C.S	
	2.6.17		Training. 25 O.R. proceeded for attachment to 47th Field C. & R.E	
	3.6.17	11.00am	Voluntary Church Parade - Rest.	
	4.6.17		Training. 1 O.R. proceeded to III Army Rest Camp	
	5.6.17		Training. CAPT M.R. MITCHELL & 2/Lt T.L. JONES to Hospital	
	6.6.17		Training. 420 O.R. carrying working parties to front line system CAMBRAI Rd SECTOR	
	7.6.17		" 360. O.R. " " " "	
	8.6.17		" 360. O.R. wiring & digging " " "	
			LT. COL. L.L. BILTON to Hospital. CAPT A.V. ROWE assumed command of the Battn	
	9.6.17		Training. 200. O.R. carrying & working parties to front line system CAMBRAI Rd SECTOR	
			1 O.R. evacuated to C.C.S. 2nd Lt C.A. UNDERWOOD to Hospital	
	10.6.17	7.30pm	Battalion moved into huts at SIMENCOURT. 61st DIVISION in rest.	
	11.6.17		Rest & clean up. 4 O.R. evacuated to Base	
	12.6.17		Training. 1 O.R. evacuated to Base	
	13.6.17		" 3 O.R " " C.C.S. 2 O.R. evacuated to Base	

Army Form C. 2118.

WAR DIARY
or
INTELLIGENCE SUMMARY.

(Erase heading not required.) 2/8 B.N WORCESTERSHIRE REG.T (T.F)

Instructions regarding War Diaries and Intelligence Summaries are contained in F. S. Regs., Part II. and the Staff Manual respectively. Title pages will be prepared in manuscript.

Place	Date	Hour	Summary of Events and Information	Remarks and references to Appendices
FRANCE	14.6.17		Training. 2.LT M.K. BUTLER rejoined the Batt.	
	15.6.17		" 2"LT E. CROSS-BUCHANAN rejoined Batt. 2"LT C.G. CRICK to Hosp.	
	16.6.17		" 2. O.R evacuated to C.C.S	
	17.6.17		Brigade Sports. 1 O.R killed. 1 O.R evacuated. Brigade Church Parade	
	18.6.17		Training. N.o 3923 R.S.M. RANDLE.T. promoted to 2/7.St WORCS REG.T to take up a commission.	
	19.6.17		Training. 1 O.R evacuated to C.C.S	
	20.6.17		" CAPT. H.R. MITCHELL & LT J.B. GRAHAM rejoined from Hospital. 3.O.R from Base	
	21.6.17		" LT. COL. L.L. BURTON rejoined from Hospital. 2. O.R evacuated to C.C.S.	
	22.6.17	7.36am	Batt.n marched to GOUY-EN-ARTOIS entrained there and detrained at HESDIN at 5 p.m and marched to Billets at LINZEUX	
	23.6.17		Rest & clean up	
	24.6.17	10.30am	Church parade. CAPT A. CLIFF rejoined Batt. 3. O.R evacuated to C.C.S	
	25.6.17		Training	
	26.6.17		Training. 1. O.R evacuated to C.C.S	
	27.6.17		Training. 2.O.R joined from Base, 1 O.R evacuated to C.C.S. 1 O.R to ENGLAND for commission	

Army Form C. 2118.

WAR DIARY
or
INTELLIGENCE SUMMARY.
(Erase heading not required.) 2/8TH BN WORCESTERSHIRE REGT (T.F.)

Place	Date	Hour	Summary of Events and Information	Remarks and references to Appendices
FRANCE	28.6.17		Training. 2/Lt C.C. ORICK rejoined 18th from Hospital. Capt W.M. CORNELIUS R.A.M.C. rejoined 18th from Base. Capt R.D. MOORE R.A.M.C. rejoined 2/3 D Field Ambulance	
	29.6.17		Training. I.O.R evacuated to C.C.S	
	30.6.17		183rd BRIGADE Horse Show & Sports	A.V. Ross Capt for O.C. 2/8 Worcs.

2/8TH WORCESTERS.

Vol 15

WAR DIARY.

JULY 1917

Army Form C. 2118.

WAR DIARY
or
INTELLIGENCE SUMMARY.
(Erase heading not required.)   2/8 Bn WORCESTERSHIRE REGT (T.F.)

Instructions regarding War Diaries and Intelligence Summaries are contained in F.S. Regs., Part II. and the Staff Manual respectively. Title pages will be prepared in manuscript.

Place	Date	Hour	Summary of Events and Information	Remarks and references to Appendices
FRANCE	1.7.17		G.O.C. 61st Division presented M.C. ribbons to Lt R.M. STALLARD & 2/Lt I.G. PRITCHARD and M.M. ribbons to Serg E. GEORGE, Sgt J. TARRANT & No. 241869 Pte R.T.S. PARSONS	
	2.7.17		2. O.R. from Base	
	3.7.17		Training. Batt Competitions. 1 O.R. evacuated to C.C.S	
	"		" " A/Major H.W. DAVIES rejoined Bn from Senior Officers School at ALDERSHOT	
	4.7.17		Training - Battalion competitions	
	5.7.17		Battalion attack & wood-fighting at WAIL. 1 O.R. to 183rd L.T.M's	
	6.7.17		Training in open warfare. Final of L.G. competition. 1 O.R. evacuated to C.C.S	
	7.7.17		Training, 1 Batt. Cooking Competition. Lt GEO GRAHAM proceeded on 7 days leave	
	8.7.17		34 O.R's Divn Baths. Batt. Cooking Competition	
	9.7.17		Training in open warfare. 1/Lt M.K. BUTLER to C.C.S	
	10.7.17		Training	
	11.7.17		Open warfare attack on WAIL area. 2 Lt W.E. TURNER to C.C.S. Lt EL RABONE appointed G.S.O.3 to 56th Div.	
	12.7.17		Training	

Army Form C. 2118.

WAR DIARY
or
INTELLIGENCE SUMMARY.
(Erase heading not required.)

Instructions regarding War Diaries and Intelligence Summaries are contained in F. S. Regs., Part II. and the Staff Manual respectively. Title pages will be prepared in manuscript.

Place	Date	Hour	Summary of Events and Information	Remarks and references to Appendices
FRANCE	13.7.17		Open warfare attack in WAIL area. A/Capt S PRITCHARD to CCS, 1 OR	
			transferred to 25 1st Employ Co.	
	14.7.17		Training. 5 OR's from Base. 1 OR to CCS.	
	15.7.17		Church Parade. 3 OR to CCS	
	16.7.17		Training. Trench to trench attack. 3 OR's from Base	
	17.7.17		do Lt H R HOLCROFT to hospital. 1 OR to CCS	
	18.7.17		do	
	19.7.17		do Divisional Row Meeting. 2 OR's to C.C.S. Wet	
	20.7.17		Trench to trench attack in WAIL. A/Capt C PRITCHARD rejoined from hospital.	
	21.7.17		Training	
	22.7.17		Church Parade. Capt H R MITCHELL to England. 4 OR B C SS	
	23.7.17		Training. 6 OR BCSS 1 OR to Div Train	
	24.7.17		Trench to trench attack – 2/Lt W E TURNER rejoined battalion from Hospital	
	25.7.17		Battalion less A Coy left LINZEUX at 1.20 AM and marched to PETIT HOUVIN where it entrained arriving at 6.45. Reached ESQUELBECQ at 9'40 and marched to billets at ZEGGARS CAPEL - very hot.	

T2134. Wt. W708—776. 500000. 4/15. Sir J. C. & S.

Army Form C. 2118.

WAR DIARY
or
INTELLIGENCE SUMMARY.
(Erase heading not required.)

Instructions regarding War Diaries and Intelligence Summaries are contained in F.S. Regs., Part II. and the Staff Manual respectively. Title pages will be prepared in manuscript.

Place	Date	Hour	Summary of Events and Information	Remarks and references to Appendices
FRANCE	26/7/17		A Coy entrained at PETIT HOUVIN at 10.45 AM and reached billets at ZEGGERS CAPEL at 11 A.M. Remainder of Battalion cleaning up and entrng 4DPoH CCS	
	27/7/17		Training in inspection of billets	
	28/7/17		do	
	29/7/17		Inoculation in morning. Draft of 115 O.R. from Base	
	30/7/17		West Riding - 70 O.R. just sworn at 5th ARMY Rockets School. Bombing war started at Brigade	
	31/7/17		Training. Reconnoitred land to bend attack on ERINGHEM area	

Arthur Capt & Adj
for O.C.
2/4th Batt. Monmouthshire Regt

T2134. Wt. W708—776. 500000. 4/15. Sir J. C. & S.

16.B

Vol 17

Sept. 1917

War Diary
of
2/8th Bt. The Worcestershire Regt.

15.B

Vol 16

August 1917

War Diary
of
2/8th Bn. The Worcestershire Regt

WAR DIARY
INTELLIGENCE SUMMARY

Army Form C. 2118.

Place	Date	Hour	Summary of Events and Information	Remarks and references to Appendices
FRANCE	Aug 1		Billets at ZEGGARS CAPELL. Beyond. No training. Lt R W STEVENSON reported from 1st WORCESTERS. 1 O R to CCS	
	2		Bn rest. CAPT CLIFF proceeded to ETAPLES as a draft-conducting officer. 2Lt T G PLAYER joined Bn.	
	3		Bn rested. 2nd Bn. SIR AYLMER HUNTER-WESTON K.C.B. Divn commanding 1st Corps broke Lt Hale	
	4		Sick wd. 2Lt RB FORSYTH joined Bn	
	5		Health Baths. Divine Service	
	6		Coy training. 5th Army B.F. Intate worked Bn. 1 O R to CCS	
	7		Bde Trench attack on ERIN SHIP M. area. A noncomgnd officer	
	8		Coy training. Lt J F BOMFORD to Hospital	
	9		Coy training. 4 O R from Base	
	10		Bade trench to head attack	
	11		Visited by Lt GEN SIR WATTS commanding XIX Corps visited Bn.	
	12		Divine Service. 3 O R from Base. 3 O R to CCS.	
	13		2 Lt HANCOCK joined from Base. 3 O R to CCS. 2 Lt LOCKWOOD to Depot K	

Army Form C. 2118.

WAR DIARY
OR
INTELLIGENCE SUMMARY.
(Erase heading not required.)

Instructions regarding War Diaries and Intelligence Summaries are contained in F. S. Regs., Part II. and the Staff Manual respectively. Title pages will be prepared in manuscript.

Place	Date	Hour	Summary of Events and Information	Remarks and references to Appendices
FRANCE	Aug 15		Preparing for move. 10 O.R. to C.C.S.	
			Bn. formed up 3 A.M. marched to ESQUELBECQ and entrained. Detrained at	
			POPERINGHE and marched to B RANHOEK area	
	16		Marched to Bivouac at GOLDFISH CHATEAU 1 mile W. of YPRES	MAP L.
			Battalion had few shares	
	17		Relieved 10th R.I.R. in support trenches. Completed at 5.30 pm. Throughout relieved 9th R.I.R. in	
			front line (C + D in front A + B in support) Relief complete at 12.30 am 18 inst. Corps Reinforcement -	
			supplied drew + transport R.H.Q at YPRES NORTH. Trench strength 584. 2 o.r. wounded.	
	18		During night 17/18 got lined on left with 11th Glos. line. On the night 9/10 N.L.I not in touch	
			but in front their position some 500ˣ in rear of our. 1 o.r. missing believed killed 3 o.r. wounded.	
	19		Very heavy shelling both by day + night. Right of 10/19th established joint post with 9/10 "H.L.I	
			Dry advanced line to end of redoubt on our line. 6 o.r. killed 14 o.r. wounded.	
	20		Shelling very heavy at stand to morning through and continuous intercommunication	
			shelling during rest of day + night. Closed a post of 20 Bosch from our right	
			flank + advanced our front post. o.r. wounded 5	
	21		Night of 20/21st dug another line in front of our view line. Relief by 84 Brocks on left	

WAR DIARY or INTELLIGENCE SUMMARY

Army Form C. 2118.

(Erase heading not required.)

Place	Date	Hour	Summary of Events and Information	Remarks and references to Appendices
	1917 Aug 21		and 7th Cameron in reserve. Relief complete at 11.30 am. Returned to YPRES NORTH Camp. 1 OR missing 2 OR wounded (1 accidentally)	
	22		During afternoon our Camp was shelled by H.V. gun, shells coming in pairs at about an hours interval causing a few casualties. 1 O.R. Killed 6 O.R. wounded	
	23		In camp preparing at 1 hours notice to go up to the line. Enemy h.v. not again shelled the Camp. Capt GOODALL to C.C.S.	
	24		Relieved the 7th WORCESTERS in support line (old British front line trench) with Bat. H.Q. at WARWICK FARM	
	25		Worked in support trench improving it and making shelters. do. 1. OR killed 10 R wounded	
	26		At 8.30 pm moved up to front and relieved 7th WORCESTERS. B Company on left A Company on right. D Company divided into two parties, detailed to attack AISNE Ho. & TRENCH and GALLIPOLI. C Company in reserve in old German Lane.	
	27		At Before daybreak A. B. & D Companies pushed up forming up on their marks preparatory to attacking. Continued thus after day light mean by many	

WAR DIARY
or
INTELLIGENCE SUMMARY.
(Erase heading not required.)

Army Form C. 2118.

Place	Date	Hour	Summary of Events and Information	Remarks and references to Appendices
	1917 Aug 27		any advanced position on which tapes & Ram very heavy last night & today. At 1.50 pm our Barrage Started and we advanced to the attack. Tps got on well but centre did not get forward. Party for GALLIPOLI got held up but Barn on Short night did not get forward. Withdrew in good order to SOMME line. Reserve Company pushed forward to Regt Bivvy back. KILLED:- 2/LT. T.G.G. CRICK. 2/LT W.E. TURNER. 2/LT R.H. HANCOCK. 35 O.Rs. WOUNDED:- CAPT G.T. PRITCHARD (at duty.) CAPT H. LEVERS. CAPT C.W. HOLCROFT. 2/LC.J. HULL. CAPT W.H. CORNELIUS. 99 O.Rs. 4. O.Rs missing believed killed.	MAP. M
	28		During the night one company of 7th Worcs pushed up to relieve outpost line. Enemy shelled all dugouts & tracks heavily. Pushed down PLUM. UHLAN and JASPAR FARMS. 1 O.R Killed 1 Wounded	
	29/29		Brigade arranged joint Bn of 7th & 8th Worc. advanced hdqtrs under O.C. 8th and troops on O.B.L. under command of O.C. 7. 4 Wabour 6th Worc. took over outpost line again	
VLAMERTINGHE	29/30 30/31		Both Bns relieved by 6th & 7th WARWICK's. 8th returned to 'B' Camp near VLAMERTINGHE. 31st Rested, cleaning & reorganising	

J. A. Honora Delton
Lt. Col.
Comdg 4th Bttn Worc. Regt.

Army Form C. 2118.

WAR DIARY
or
INTELLIGENCE SUMMARY.
(Erase heading not required.)

2/8 WORCESTERSHIRE REGT

Place	Date	Hour	Summary of Events and Information	Remarks and references to Appendices
FRANCE	1917 Sept 19		Marched to camp at SYMENCOURT arriving at 3.30am on 20th	
	20		Company training. LT(A/Capt) H. LEVERS awarded MILITARY CROSS	
	21		— do — 2/Lt R.C.P. HODGSON to hospital. 4 O.R. arrived from base.	
	22		— do — Officers visited front line GREENLAND HILL sector - right sub section	
	23		Battalion marched to GRIMSBY CAMP, ST NICOLAS	
	24		Battalion moved into line in GREENLAND HILL sector - right sub section taking over from the 9th Bn East Yorks. Relief took place without incident. Into the line.	Disposition map enclosed
	25		In line. Day quiet except for a Lt.T.M. shelling Gravette. 2 O.R. Killed 3 slightly wounded.	
	26		do do 3 O.R. wounded 2/Lts W.J.B. LT J.F. BONFIELD from leave.	
	27		do Rather more shelling to reserve line & trestle way from 2 O.R.'s wounded 11.15 p.m.	
	28		CHILD very slightly wounded at duty). Pte TAYLOR dead & interred. In line. Shelled (Chili) AVENUE & CAULDRON followed by considerable bay fire.	
	29		Heavy shelling on CAULDRON throwing [illegible] & casualties & crater built challenge. 5p.m. 2nd Lt I AM at Evans buried by 7 M/s & a shelling was put in front line	
	30		and the enemy were seen lining up on No Mans land. They were driven off by M.G. fire and L.G. fire. 6 O.R. wounded. In the evening we were relieved by 2/7 WORCESTERS without incident—	

J.B. Graham Capt & Major
Comdg. 2/8th Bn. Worc. Regt.

Army Form C. 2118.

WAR DIARY
OF
INTELLIGENCE SUMMARY. 2/8 Worcestershire Regt
(Erase heading not required.)

Instructions regarding War Diaries and Intelligence Summaries are contained in F.S. Regs., Part II. and the Staff Manual respectively. Title pages will be prepared in manuscript.

Place	Date	Hour	Summary of Events and Information	Remarks and references to Appendices
FRANCE	1917 Sept 12		Working parties. 1 OR killed. 1 OR wounded (at duty)	
	13		Returned to No 2 BRANDHOEK and camp for the night. Left CANAL BANK at 9.30am. 1 O.R. from C.R.S. 2 OR to C.C.S.	
	14		Moved at 9.30 am to No 3 WATOU AREA. 2 OR to C.C.S.	
	15		Reorganising, fitting out, training. 2/Lt P. Merifield. 2/Lt J.H. Rose. 2/Lt W. Hall. 2/Lt W. Rundle. 2/Lt G.A. Gale. 2/Lt S. Harrison. Lt N.V.H. Symons M.C. joined Battalion from Divisional Depot Bn. 2/Lt W. Hall to Hospital.	
	16		Company Church Parade. 2/Lt J. Parkes and 1 O.R. from Base. 1 OR from 17 C.C.S. No 24 1086 Pte C Griffiths awarded military medal	
	17		Battalion marched to WEMAERS CAPPEL.	
	18		Company specialist training. Military medal awarded to No 241211 Cpl E.H. Jones No 242537 4/C J.N. Vickers. No 240950 Pte J.E. Torns. No 242250 Cpl Portman. No 240726 Pte A. Grinnell. No 241963 Pte T. Hackett. No 241996 Pte Pleace. No 241902 4/C E.W. Smith. No 241967 Pte J. Yoaden. No 242133 Pte G. Williams. No 242220 Pte G. Reynolds. No 242067 Pte J.E. Lewis.	
	19		Battalion marched to CASSEL STATION Entrained at 4.21pm Detrained at ARRAS and	

Army Form C. 2118.

WAR DIARY
or
INTELLIGENCE SUMMARY. 2/8 WORCESTERSHIRE REGT
(Erase heading not required.)

Instructions regarding War Diaries and Intelligence Summaries are contained in F.S. Regs., Part II. and the Staff Manual respectively. Title pages will be prepared in manuscript.

Place	Date	Hour	Summary of Events and Information	Remarks and references to Appendices
FRANCE	1917 Sept. 1		Company Training and Baths. 1 O.R. to C.C.S.	
	2		Memorial Service for those recently killed in action. 3 O.R. to C.C.S. 1 O.R. to C.S.D. 4 O.R. returned from C.R.S.	
	3		Company Training and Medical Inspection. Camp was lightly shelled at night no casualties. 1 O.R. to C.C.S. — 2 O.R. returned from C.R.S.	
	4		Company Training 1 O.R. to C.R.S.	
	5		—d— (Anniversary of formation of Battalion - Dinner -) 3 O.R. to C.S.D.	
	6		—d—	
	7		—d— Shelter Board party of 50 men sent up to front line at WIELTJE. 2/Lt H. L. GERALD; E.A. BROWN H.S. BELL C.S.S. JACKSON joined from 61st Div Depot Batt on 28/8/17 Lt A.F. FRANKLIN joined from 48th Div Depot Batt on 29/8/17	
	8		Went up to YPRES CANAL BANK in reserve and took over from 7 R Worcesters at 9.30 p.m. Fifty men attached to R.E's at CANAL BANK and in YPRES. 2 O.R. to C.C.S. 1 to Gen. Hos.	
	9		Working parties to front and support lines. Transport lines bombed & shelled. 1 O.R. to C.C.S. 1 O.R. to C.R.S. 1 O.R. killed 6 O.R. wounded (2 Shell Shock)	
	10		1 O.R. to C.C.S	
	11		—d— Transport lines again bombed & shelled. 1 O.R. to C.C.S.B	

T.2134. Wt. W708—776. 500000. 4/15. Sir J. C. & S.

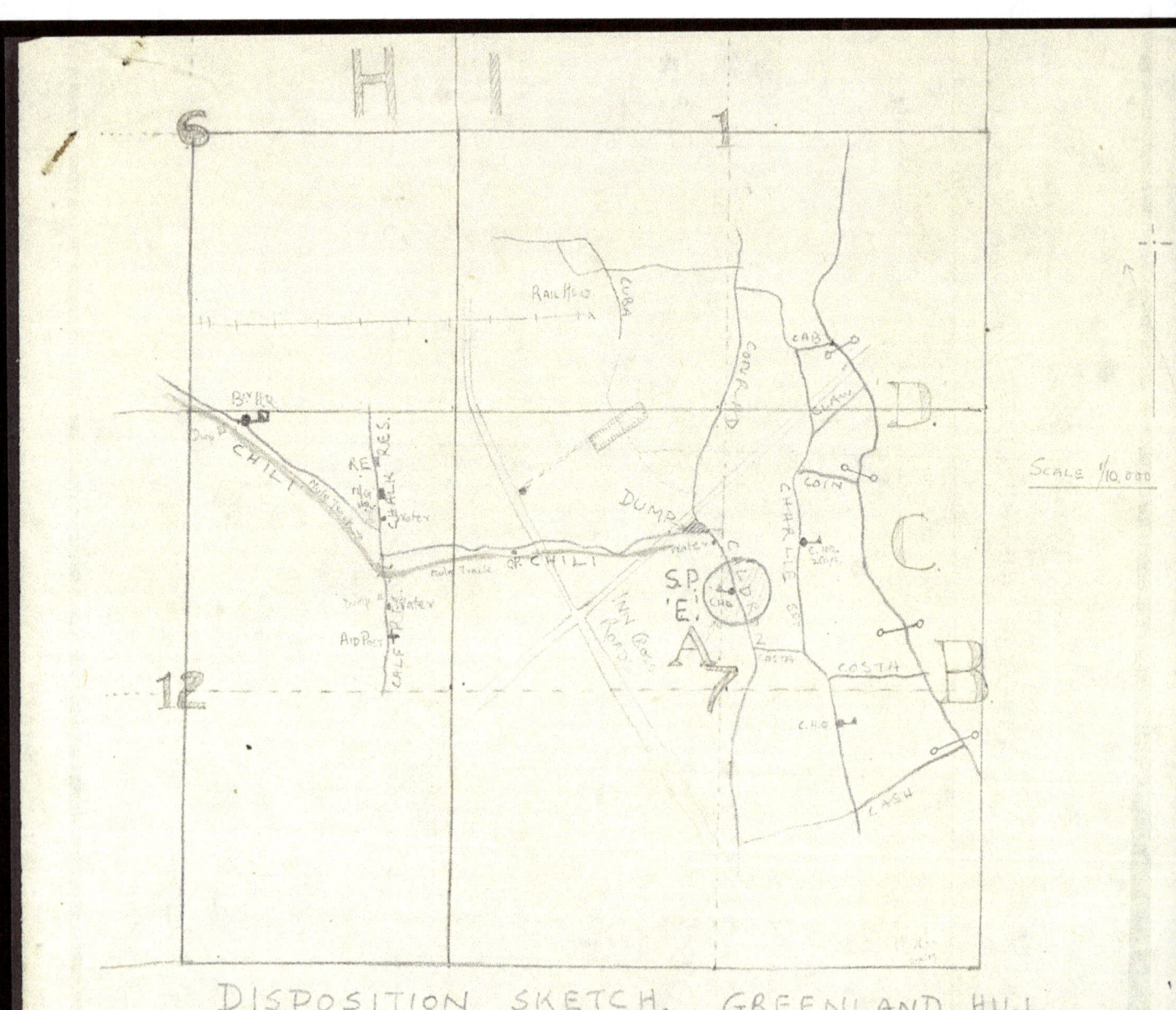

DISPOSITION SKETCH. GREENLAND HILL.

Vol 18

17.B

October 1917

War Diary of

2/8th Batt. The Worcestershire Regt.

Army Form C. 2118.

WAR DIARY
INTELLIGENCE SUMMARY.
(Erase heading not required.)

2/8 WORCESTERSHIRE REGT

Instructions regarding War Diaries and Intelligence Summaries are contained in F. S. Regs., Part II. and the Staff Manual respectively. Title pages will be prepared in manuscript.

Place	Date	Hour	Summary of Events and Information	Remarks and references to Appendices
FRANCE	Oct 1		In support trenches in GAVRELLE SWITCH. Working parties, weather fine	Thurs
	2		do	Fri
			at 2/4 PARKES	
	3		Transferred to 1/7 Worcs Regt. 1 OR to Base	Sat
			do	
	4		do	Sun
			1 Lt HODGSON wounded. Bn moved	
			to GRIMSBY CAMP, ST NICHOLAS being relieved by 4/5th GLOSTERS	
	5		To GRIMSBY CAMP cleaning up. CAPT CODSALL rejoined – 11 OR joined	Mon
	6		from Div Dept	Tues
			Baths and trainings. weather brisk.	
	7		Lost. Brune serm. 12.0 R from 6 am	Wed
	8		Training & working parties. weather bad w sen	Thurs
	9		do	Fri
	10		do	Sat
	11		do	Sun
	12		do 30 OR to CCS	Mon
	13		Muskets & working parties weather brisk	Tues

Army Form C. 2118.

WAR DIARY
or
INTELLIGENCE SUMMARY.
(Erase heading not required.)

2/8 WORCESTERSHIRE REGT

Place	Date	Hour	Summary of Events and Information	Remarks and references to Appendices
FRANCE	Col/14		During serves furnished working parties weather fine 2/1st T.W.F.RY joined	Fine
	15		weather very fine	
			Training working parties	
	16		Relieved 2/5th WARWICKS on night Sub Sector of CHEMICAL WORKS SECTOR (ARRAS) relief complete at 10.10pm	1 OR to C.C.S.
			Dispositions as per appendix	Map N.
	17		In the line. Weather fine. Enemy party quiet CORONA SUPPORT shelled { 2 OR WOUNDED. 2 OR MISSING 1 OR to C.C.S	
	18		" " " do also CORFU. 1 OR to Base (neigh) 1 OR to C.C.S	LT N.V.H. Symons wounded
	19		" " " Enemy mine before CORONA. CORFU & CHEMICAL party heavily shelled	
	20		" " " enemy greater activity R.B. FORSYTH to England (Sick) 1 OR to C.C.S.	
	21		" " " some heavy reply to our T.M shoot	
	22		" " " do	Lt N.V.H. Symons to England 1 OR wounded
	22		Relieved by 2/6 WORCESTERS in the front line. B Coy remaining in support. Relief complete 8.15 pm. A Coy went to cellars in FAMPOUX. C. & D with Bat HQ to PUDDING TRENCH about 1 mile north of FAMPOUX on the Arras road	
	23		Working parties & training, rending party	
	24		do Very heavy bombardment by our artillery. 2 rending parties	

Army Form C. 2118.

WAR DIARY
or
INTELLIGENCE SUMMARY.
(Erase heading not required.)   2/8 WORCESTERSHIRE REGT

Instructions regarding War Diaries and Intelligence Summaries are contained in F.S. Regs., Part II. and the Staff Manual respectively. Title pages will be prepared in manuscript.

Place	Date	Hour	Summary of Events and Information	Remarks and references to Appendices
1917 Oct	24		went over Eur Support Coy avy very heavily shelled. 1 OR killed 1 wounded. Rain	
	25		Working parties & training. Weather bad	
	26		" " heavy rain	
	27		" " Weather much improved	
	28		Relieved 2/7 Worcs. Regt in right sub sector of CHEMICAL WORKS SECTOR relief completed 6.55 p.m. Disposition as on 16th inst except that one Company of 2/7th relieved B Coy in 'A' & 'B' pots. CORDITE. B Coy going to PUDDING TRENCH	
	29		In the line. Enemy fairly quiet but jumpy. Weather fine. Capt C.W. HOLCROFT reported sick. 1 OR to C.C.S. 3 OR wounded	
	30		-do- enemy artillery fairly active. Weather fine. 2 OR wounded	
	31		-do- -do-	

J Edward Dillon
Lieut-Col.
Cmdg 2/8th Bn Worcestershire Regt.

2/8th Bn. Worcestershire Regt.

War Diary.

WAR DIARY
or
INTELLIGENCE SUMMARY.   2/8 WORCESTERSHIRE REGT

Army Form C. 2118.

Place	Date	Hour	Summary of Events and Information	Remarks and references to Appendices
FRANCE	1917 Nov 1		In the Line – Enemy quiet. Weather fine	
	2		– do – Enemy more active	1 O.R. to C.C.S.
	3		– do – Enemy quiet. Relieved by 2/7 Worcesters two Companies 1st Bn H.Q at PUDDING TRENCH 1 Company at FAMPOUX and 1 Company at SINGLE ARCH – CORDITE & CRETE trenches. Relief complete 6.30 p.m. 2/Lt G.W. PALMER - G.L. MARTIN and J.A. GREAVES joined from 61st Div Depot Bat. 2/Lt S. HARRISON to hospital 2 O.R. to C.C.S.	
	4		Nothing further	
	5		do Baths 2/Lt G.W. PALMER to hospital. LT H.M. ADAMS joined from 183rd L.T. M.B.	1 O.R. to C.C.S.
	6		Nothing further. Baths	
	7		do do	
	8		do do	
	9		Battalion Relieved by 2/5 Bn GLOUCESTERSHIRE REGT Moved into LEVIS BARRACKS. ARRAS	
	10		Rest. 2/Lt G PALMER rejoined from hospital	
	11		Working parties & Church parade	
	12		Training	

Army Form C.2118.

WAR DIARY
or
INTELLIGENCE SUMMARY.
(Erase heading not required.)

2/8 WORCESTERSHIRE REGT

Place	Date	Hour	Summary of Events and Information	Remarks and references to Appendices
FRANCE	1917 May 13		Working parties - Musketry training	
	14		do	
	15		do	Raid on enemy trenches east of FAMPOUX Res Offensive Novelea
			Notes N° 28 attached also copy Report on raid. Killed O.R. 3 Missing O.R. 1 Wounded 2/Lt F.W. Oxley 28 & report
			F.R.Y. O.R. 10 (accidently) 10 R.L. C.C.S.	
	16		Working parties & Musketry training. 10TH L.C.C.S. L/Cpl R.G. FORSYTH Taken on strength of Batt.	
			Having been noted as from E. ENGLAND in error by base	
	17		Musketry training	
	18		CHURCH PARADE	
	19		Working parties. Bn Boxing Coyt. R. CLARKE Wn Heavyweight competition. Program an	
			Musketry. Best afternoon action. Best rifle firman's action. Best L.G. section. Best section.	
			Officer admitted Lt BROWN Sgt CLARKE died of wounds	
	20		Red. 10TH L.C.C.S.	
	21		Relieved 2/7 R WARWICKS in the left centre sector GREENLAND HILL Sector 1 O.R. killed	
	22		In the line. Enemy active. MILITARY MEDAL awarded to 26347 Sgt BENNETT. 241337 L/Cpl	
			(A/Cpl) A.H.G. SALISBURY 240367 Pte PITTAWAY. 241721 Pte R. WYATT. 241057 Sgt R.W.	

WAR DIARY
OF
INTELLIGENCE SUMMARY. 2/8 WORCESTERSHIRE REGT

(Erase heading not required.)

Army Form C. 2118.

Instructions regarding War Diaries and Intelligence Summaries are contained in F.S. Regs., Part II. and the Staff Manual respectively. Title pages will be prepared in manuscript.

Place	Date	Hour	Summary of Events and Information	Remarks and references to Appendices
FRANCE	1917 Nov 22		ELLIOTT. 242206 PTE J. PHILLIPS	
	23		In the line Enemy quiet. 2 OR Wounded	
	24		do. enemy quiet 2 OR Wounded	
	25		do. do.	
	26		do. do. 1 OR to C.C.S	
	27		do. enemy active Capt GOODSALL wounded. 1 OR killed 3 OR wounded	
	28		Relieved by 6/7 R.S.F. proceeded to ARRAS relief complete 1 pm	
	29		Billeted in ARRAS - ARRAS shelled 2/Lt M K BUTLER reported from our depot also	
	30	13.0.A.	2/Lt C H. ALBERT (joins from 5th NOTES) Entrained at DAINVILLE for BAPAUME to proceed to BARASTRE - Order cancelled at BAPAUME Batt entrained & proceeded to ROYAUX COURT marched to FRESCAULT transferred in HAVRIN COURT wood in reserve to GUARDS who had counterattacked the enemy	

J. Thomas Lilly
Lt Col

December 1917

War Diary

of

2/8th Bn The Worcestershire Regt.

Army Form C. 2118.

WAR DIARY
or
INTELLIGENCE SUMMARY.
(Erase heading not required.) 2/8 Bat" The Worcestershire Regiment

Instructions regarding War Diaries and Intelligence Summaries are contained in F. S. Regs., Part II. and the Staff Manual respectively. Title pages will be prepared in manuscript.

Place	Date	Hour	Summary of Events and Information	Remarks and references to Appendices
FRANCE	1917 Dec 1		Battalion moved up to the line at 5 p.m. via Beaucamp and Villers-Plouich. Two Companies in the line just south of La Vacquerie (Hindenburgh support and Front line) one Company in support and one Company in Corner Work at La Vacquerie along with Battalion HQ. Relief complete at 4.15 a.m. on 2nd inst. Relieved Buffs, R.Z. and details. 7 O.R. wounded	
	2	A.M. 6.30	Enemy attacked mainly on my right and succeeded in getting on top of Battalion on my right. Advance his attack was repulsed 4 O.R. to C.C.S.	
		P.M. 3.30	Enemy again attacked in large numbers. Attack repulsed on my front but enemy got into the old Hindenburg support front line on my right where he already held the Sap.	
		6.30	Counter attacked with my support Company. Cleared enemy from Sunken road on my right but could not clearly clear line from the trenches	
		11	2/5 Warwicks arrived to relieve us in front line: handed our front line to them & put 2 Companies in my support line ready to counter attack again at dawn. Left one Company at Corner Work and took remainder back to old Battle front H.Q. line from Village Road to Fusilier Alley. Relief complete 6.30 a.m. 3rd inst. 2/Lieut H. Gerald Killed. Capt R.H. Stallard. 2/Lieut F.A. Adams. 2/Lieut H. Merifield wounded. 2/Lieut H.S. Bell missing wounded believed prisoner 13 O.R. wounded	

Army Form C. 2118.

WAR DIARY
or
INTELLIGENCE SUMMARY.
(Erase heading not required.) 2/8 Bat The Worcestershire Regt.

Instructions regarding War Diaries and Intelligence Summaries are contained in F.S. Regs, Part II. and the Staff Manual respectively. Title pages will be prepared in manuscript.

Place	Date	Hour	Summary of Events and Information	Remarks and references to Appendices
FRANCE	1917 DEC 3	7.30 A.M.	Enemy again attacked in force especially on CORNER WORK.	
		9.30 P.M.	Sent another Company up to reinforce CORNER WORK	
		2.30	Information that enemy working round trenches in rear of CORNER WORK and up bombing nearly up to about three trenches which was successfully done – Remainder of Battalion stood to in old British front & support lines all day. Enemy shelling heavy. Enemy attack stopped we are in both trenches holding CORNER RESERVE trench.	
			Capt G. PRITCHARD killed 2/Lieut J.H. ROSE wounded, Lieut E.H.A. LOCKWOOD & Lieut E.H.G. GUMPERT wounded (gassed) 2/Lieut C.H. ALBERT missing, 2/Lieut G.L. MARTIN wounded 7 O.R. killed OR 69 O.R. wounded 10 missing wounded believed prisoner. 35 missing believed pris.	
	4		over. 7 O.R. wounded gassed 1 O.R missing believed killed. The enemy has been much in evidence by heavy artillery using a lot of gas shells.	
	5		Lt Col L.L. BILTON evacuated (gassed) at duty. 12 O.R wounded. 6 O.R. to C.C.S. Enemy machine artillery 7gas shell shower. Lt S. MILLER M.O.R.C wounded at duty. 3 O.R to C.C.S. Relieved by 2/1 BUCKS and returned to HAVRINCOURT WOOD.	
	6-9		In HAVRINCOURT WOOD reorganising and sorting parties. 1 O.R killed 18 & 1 O.R to England for Commission. 10 O.R wounded	

T2134. Wt. W708—776. 500000. 4/15. Sir J. C. & S.

Army Form C. 2118.

WAR DIARY or INTELLIGENCE SUMMARY.

(Erase heading not required.) 2/8 Bat" THE WORCESTERSHIRE R^gt

Place	Date	Hour	Summary of Events and Information	Remarks and references to Appendices
FRANCE	1917 Decr 9	pm 4.30	Moved up to support at VILLERS - PLOUICH under command of MAJOR DAVIES. 1 O.R Killed	
	10		CAPT C.W. HOLCROFT wounded at duty. 2 O.R wounded - In Support 2 O.R wounded 13 O.R. C.C.S.	
	11		Working parties to front line.	
	12		In support nothing. Parties to front line. 1 O.R to C.C.S.	
	13		Joined post of 1 officer & 60 O.R. to cover FIFTEEN RAVINE.	Sketch O
			1 O.R killed 2 O.R wounded.	
	14		Relieved by WORCESTERS, inform bus from RILEY to FORWARD TRENCH. (Disposition Sketch)	
	15		In front line 4 O.R wounded 10 O.R to C.C.S.	
	16		1 O.R to ENGLAND for commission. relieved by 2/4 BERKS & 1/4 altⁿ of 2/5 -	
	17		GLOSTERS, returned to HAVRINCOURT WOOD	
			In reserve. Very cold with snow	
	18		Hard frost (14th) 242070 P^{te} T. COLLIER. 241915 - 4/C R WINTER. 241105 -	
			P^{te} J. BRIDGES. 242166 P^{te} C.H. GARRETT. 263443 C^{pl} A.A. HUDD awarded Military	
			Medal.	
	19		Hard frost	

Army Form C. 2118.

WAR DIARY
OR
INTELLIGENCE SUMMARY.
(Erase heading not required.) 2/8 Bn The WORCESTERSHIRE REG.T

Instructions regarding War Diaries and Intelligence Summaries are contained in F. S. Regs., Part II. and the Staff Manual respectively. Title pages will be prepared in manuscript.

Place	Date	Hour	Summary of Events and Information	Remarks and references to Appendices
FRANCE	1917 Dec 20		Moved up & took over and relieved 2/4 "BERKS" Btn. Completed 7pm. Inspection sketch forwarded	Sketch P
	21		enemy quiet with sniper fairly active	
	22		In front trenches. 1 OR killed. 2 OR joined from Sig. Hospital.	
			" 2 OR to CCS. Battalion relieved by 2nd Bn RM LI and returned to	
HAYRINCOURT WOOD				
	23		Marched to MANNENCOURT & took billets.	
	24		Entrained at ETRICOURT at 8pm. detrained at PLATEAU STATION and marched to billets	
			at BRAY-SUR-SOMME. Hay transport by own half by road. Hancford 2 OR to CCS	
	25		3 OR. joined division depot. Capt C.W. HOLCROFT awarded D.S.O. Capt E.S. MITCHELL, L.T. H.M. ADAMS	
			2/Lt W HALL & 2/Lt S.S. JACKSON awarded Military Cross 241052 Sgt R.W. ELLIOTT & 241118 Cpl	
			F W KING awarded D.C.M.	
	26		Training	
	27		"	
	28		Capt S A GODSALL rejoined Bn	
	29		2/Lts R.H. HUNT, C.T. PRATT & R. TODD and 17 OR joined from div depot 152	
	30		Church Parade - New Xmas Dinner	

Army Form C. 2118.

WAR DIARY
or
INTELLIGENCE SUMMARY.   2/8th Bn THE WORCESTERSHIRE REGT
(Erase heading not required.)

Instructions regarding War Diaries and Intelligence Summaries are contained in F. S. Regs., Part II. and the Staff Manual respectively. Title pages will be prepared in manuscript.

Place	Date	Hour	Summary of Events and Information	Remarks and references to Appendices
FRANCE	1917 Dec 31		Marched to BAYENVILLERS and went into billets. Hard frost road very slippery. 1 OR to CCS J. Edward Phillips Cmdg 2/8 Worc Regt	

SKETCH P

2/8th BATTALION THE WORCESTERSHIRE REGIMENT

DISPOSITION SKETCH

for

21st – 23rd DECEMBER 1917

- A Co. IN QUARRY WITH 2 SECTIONS IN RILEY.
- B Co. POSTS 13 – 17.
- C Co. " 1 – 7 SUPPORTS IN SHELTERS AT TOP OF PARTRIDGE ROAD
- D Co. " 8 – 12 SUPPORTS

SCALE. 1:5,000.

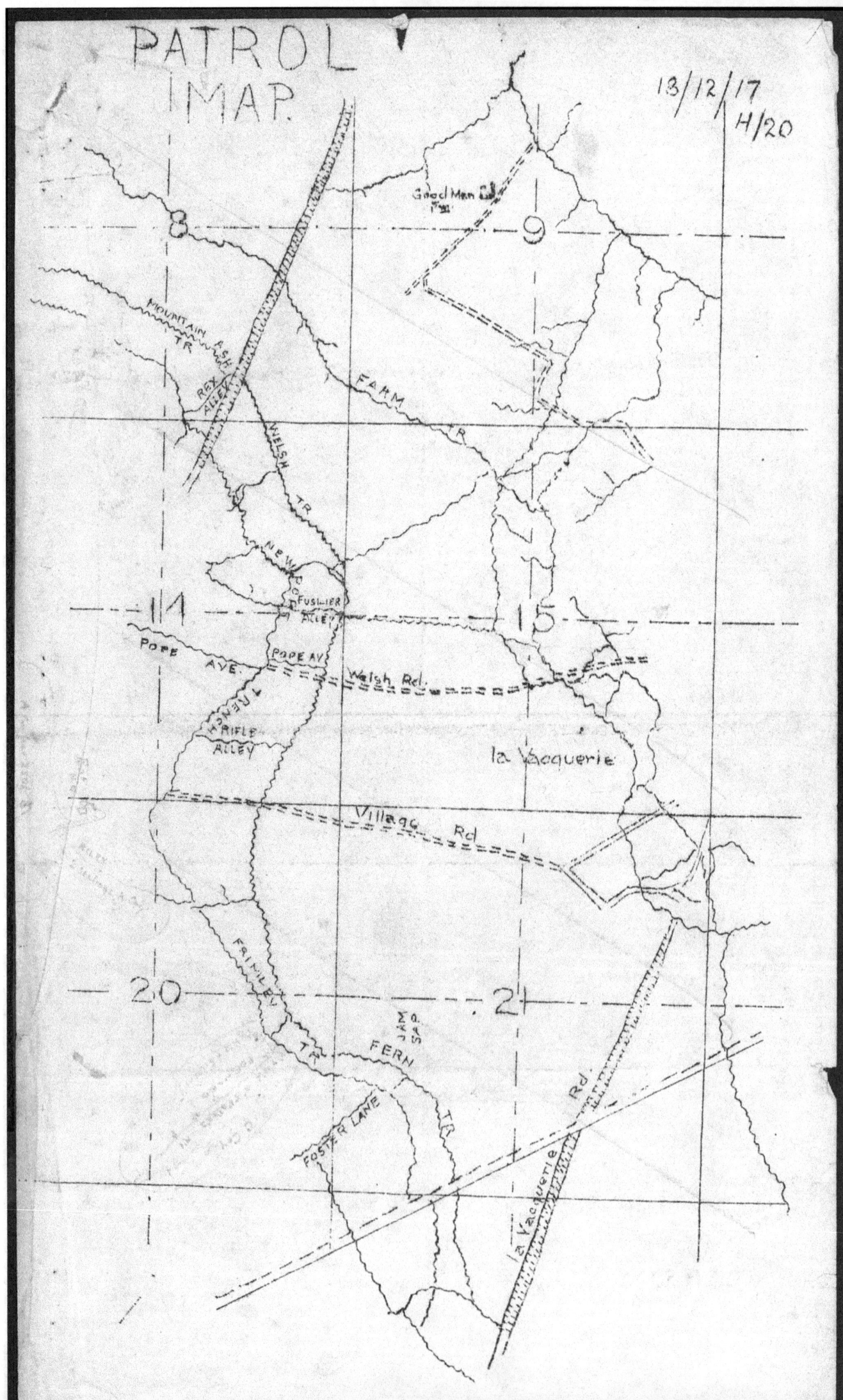

20.B.

6/3

18/61

January 1918

War Diary
of
2/8th Bn. The Worcestershire Regt

J.W.J.
1 – AUG. 1918

REGISTRY
INFANTRY RECORD OFFICE
-1 AUG 1918
WARWICK

Army Form C. 2118.

WAR DIARY
or
INTELLIGENCE SUMMARY. 2/8 B'n THE WORCESTERSHIRE Reg.t

(Erase heading not required.)

Place	Date	Hour	Summary of Events and Information	Remarks and references to Appendices
FRANCE	1918 Jan 1		Training. Reinforcement 2 O.R. from 7th Div Dept. B.n 2 O.R from C.C.S	Yes?
	2		" "	Yes?
	3		" Lieut. Butler took over command 4/P.S.T/Bde. Major Davis took B.n	Yes?
	4		" 1 O.R. to C.C.S	Yes?
	5		" Hand 144 O.R joined from Base	Yes?
	6		" 1st 40 R joined from Base. 1 O.R to C.C.S	Yes?
	7		Run and arm. Battalion marched 18 miles to CARRÉPUIS. Billeted in Lutrend.	Yes?
			one in two hours. 7 O.R to C.C.S	
	8		Hand f'n'x Battalion parade. Army Commander inspected the area.	Yes?
	9		Field arm. L.M. training	Yes?
	10		do do	Yes?
	11		Battalion marched to VUYENNES and billeted in houses and barns.	
			Received lead a reinfor. 2/Lt W RUNDLE rejoined. The following officers	
			joined the battalion. 2/Lts WELLS. YARDLEY. TURNER. SLAINDELL	
			GRINGER. FROST. SPENCELAY H. ALLARD. SUDLOW ADAMS	Yes?
			JONES LAWRENCE RUSHTON	

Army Form C. 2118.

WAR DIARY
or
INTELLIGENCE SUMMARY.
(Erase heading not required.)

Instructions regarding War Diaries and Intelligence Summaries are contained in F. S. Regs., Part II. and the Staff Manual respectively. Title pages will be prepared in manuscript.

Place	Date	Hour	Summary of Events and Information	Remarks and references to Appendices
FRANCE	Jan 12		To H/Q. 1 O R to CCS	Ap. 0
	13		Battalion marched to VAUX. Billetted in huts. Thawed.	Ap. 0
	14		Billets at GERMAINE 2/L? PARKER joined Battalion. 2 O R to CCS	Ap. 0
	15		Training ~ 2 O R to CCS	Ap. 2
	16		" 5 O R from base.	Ap. 3
	17		Rained all day	Ap. 1
	18		G.O.C. distributed honours to Officers and men. Battalion relieved 2/17 WARWICKS in right support of right sector before ST QUENTIN.	Ap. D
			bombing parties	Ap. D
	19		do do 5 O R from base	Ap. D
	20		do do	Ap. D
	21		do do	Ap. D
	22		Battalion relieved 2/17th Londons in Right sub-sector. A very quiet front for this but Shell very steady. 7 shots in front line from 2.00 to 7.00 p.m. spent. Enemy mortars about 1000 yds further back. The line is only a shallow trench but the wire is good. Relief went off well.	Ap. 3
			5 O R from base	

Army Form C. 2118.

WAR DIARY
or
INTELLIGENCE SUMMARY.
(Erase heading not required.)

Instructions regarding War Diaries and Intelligence Summaries are contained in F. S. Regs., Part II. and the Staff Manual respectively. Title pages will be prepared in manuscript.

Place	Date	Hour	Summary of Events and Information	Remarks and references to Appendices
FRANCE	23		In trenches. Very quiet. Difficult to get much work done owing to scattered shrapnel	
	24		In trenches. Our left post was raided by an enemy patrol and 2 of our men were missing. A pum pam of ours in the rear of the post & that was very quiet.	H.D
	25		In trenches. FOSSES. Very quiet.	H.D
	26		do. Relieved by 2/7th Worcesters and went into support	H.D
	27		2 O.R. wounded (accidentally)	H.D
	2		In support. FOSSES. Working parties	H.D
	28		do do	H.D
	29		do Fine and sunny. Slight frost. Working parties	H.D
	30		Relieved 2/4 Lond Regt in the right sub sector of right sector. Dispositions the same as before. Patrolling active but saw nothing of the enemy	H.D
	31		In line. Very FOSSES. Patrols of ours went over to their wire. Casualties nil.	H.D

L.S. Lieut Major
Commanding 2/8th Lond Regt

(d) From 10-30 A.M. to 2-30 P.M. animals were being watered in Sumaikchah village within 1 mile of where bodies were found. The 2 platoon water piquets were even nearer. They heard nothing.

(e) Adjt. 47th Sikhs rode back along line from Sumaikchah station for about 3 miles to meet telephone trolley at 2 P.M. He heard no firing.

3. *Wind.*—There was a fairly strong southerly breeze all day.

4. *Search*—(a) By 3 P.M. piquets having seen nothing of party, at 3-45 Captain Phelps was sent out with all sowars to meet them. He returned at 9-0 P.M. having seen no trace of them.

(b) At 6 P.M. a company was sent into village accompanied by A. P. O.

5. *Information by Mahawil.*—A. P. O. returned 9 P.M. and gave information that Shaikh Mohd. Juwad of Sumaikchah had stated that whole party had been killed by Khasraj about middle of day.

No explanation had been given of why no report was made by him to troops who were watering close to his house from 11 A.M. to 3 P.M.

6. *Bodies.*—Seventeen of the bodies were found early next morning, others were found later. All were partly stripped and most were partly buried. 17 were lying together (*i.e.* within 100 yards circle) within 100 yards of brick bridge and all close to the Dujail (a 12' nullah with 10' perpendicular banks dry here).

Lt. Stables' horse was lying about 200 yds. from ridge on west. The body of the havildar was 400 yds. east of bridge. Two bodies were found 1 mile north of bridge east of canal. Bullet wounds were only found on four corpses. All corpses bore marks of stabbing and bludgeoning. Only 3 empty cartridge cases could be found after careful search. Two men (wounded by bullets) had first field dressings on. A third used dressing was found close to the bodies.

7. *Medical Opinion.*—Medical opinion of M. O. who examined bodies early on 14th is that the men were killed on evening of 13th.

* * * * * * * *

Note.—The Medical Officer, 47th Sikhs, in his report after examination of the bodies states that in his opinion Lieut. Stables was killed by a blow of a heavy club.

CONCLUSIONS.

11. With reference to these facts the great difficulty of ascertaining the whole of the truth is apparent.

12. It is to the interest of all Arab witnesses to conceal their knowledge.

13. It is to the interest of all Mahawil—

(a) To plead ignorance in excuse for not having prevented the outrage, nor even made any report to our troops (who were in the village from 10 A.M. onwards) until questioned by A. P. O. after 6 P M., when it was evident Riat Shaikh Juwad at least had a very shrewd idea of what had happened.

(b) Lest punishment should fall on them for assisting or harbouring culprits, to make out that all connected with outrage had fled, and that those actually caught in Khasraj houses were innocent members of other tribes.

(c) Knowing that Khasraj were in disgrace and would not be able to return to claim their property, to admit a minimum of Khasraj property in the village, and have as little as possible destroyed by us; the remainder falling automatically to them free.

14. The following points however seem sufficiently established:—

(a) The party was collected together, and all were off their guard when attacked.

(b) The party was overwhelmed suddenly from close quarters.

(c) Almost all were killed by stabbing or stunning weapons quickly and at very close quarters.

(d) They had no time to use their own rifles.

(e) Three men were killed at some distance from the rest, all three from bullet wounds.

(f) Their murderers attempted to conceal the bodies, but had not time to do this thoroughly.

Other points which seem probable are—

(g) That the attack took place before midday and that all were dead before 2 P M.

(h) That the inhabitants of Sumaikchah, certainly the Shaikh, could not have been in ignorance of what was taking place.

APPENDIX VIII.

Headquarters, III Division,
12th May 1917.

Circular memorandum.

Circular Memorandum No. A-4-126, dated 26th October 1916, is cancelled and the following substituted :—

Each man will be personally responsible for the safe custody of his own rifle.

Before lying down to sleep he will attach the rifle to his person.

Except on guard, when engaged on active operations or when given special permission by the Commanding Officer, the bolt will be removed from the rifle and kept by the man in his pocket or other safe place, which will ensure that it will not be left behind if the unit has to turn out hurriedly.

The above orders will be read to the troops once a month.

www.ingramcontent.com/pod-product-compliance
Lightning Source LLC
Chambersburg PA
CBHW081430160426
43193CB00013B/2237